Personal Financial Literacy

SECOND EDITION

Joan S. Ryan

Clackamas Community College

SOUTH-WESTERN
CENGAGE Learning

Australia • Brazil • Japan • Korea • Mexico • Singapore • Spain • United Kingdom • United States

SOUTH-WESTERN
CENGAGE Learning

ISBN-13: 978-0-840-05865-2
ISBN-10: 0-840-05865-9

South-Western Cengage Learning
5191 Natorp Boulevard
Mason, OH 45040
USA

Cengage Learning is a leading provider of customized learning solutions with office locations around the globe, including Singapore, the United Kingdom, Australia, Mexico, Brazil, and Japan. Locate your local office at: **international.cengage.com/region**.

Cengage Learning products are represented in Canada by Nelson Education, Ltd.

For your course and learning solutions, visit **school.cengage.com**.

Visit our company website at **www.cengage.com**.

Printed in the United States of America
4 5 6 7 8 9 10   17 16 15 14 13

CONTENTS

CHAPTER 5 The Banking System

CHAPTER 6 Personal Risk Management

CHAPTER 7 Buying Decisions

CHAPTER 8 Preserving Your Credit

CHAPTER 9 Credit Problems and Laws

CHAPTER 10 Basics of Saving and Investing

CHAPTER 11 Saving and Investing Options

CHAPTER 12 Buying and Selling Investments

TO THE STUDENT

This student workbook is designed to accompany the *Personal Financial Literacy* student textbook. The workbook includes activities for each chapter in the textbook. Complete these activities when assigned by your instructor to review the content of each topic as you study it or when preparing for a chapter test.

The following kinds of assignments are provided in the student workbook:

- **Review of Chapter Key Terms**

  These are matching exercises in which you will review the meaning of key terms used in the chapter.

- **True/False and Multiple Choice Questions**

  True/False and Multiple Choice questions will help you assess your understanding of the topics presented throughout the chapter.

- **Building Communications Skills**

  Listening, reading, writing, and speaking exercises will help you build skill in these areas. For example, in listening activities, you will listen to your teacher or a classmate read a passage and then will answer questions related to the passage.

- **Building Math Skills**

  You will build basic math skills by completing problems related to the chapter content.

- **Careers**

  These exercises will introduce you to helpful information about careers, career searches, job opportunities, and the job market.

- **Activities Related to Content**

  Activities will allow you to apply content from the chapter or extend learning beyond what was covered in the chapter.

CHAPTER 1
How Your Choices Affect Income

EXERCISE 1-1 Review of Chapter Key Terms

Directions: Write the letter of the correct definition beside its corresponding term.

_____ 1. business cycle

_____ 2. demand

_____ 3. economy

_____ 4. ethics

_____ 5. goal

_____ 6. hard skills

_____ 7. headhunter

_____ 8. job description

_____ 9. job interview

_____ 10. job shadowing

_____ 11. references

_____ 12. resume

_____ 13. scholarship

_____ 14. skill set

_____ 15. social network

_____ 16. soft skills

_____ 17. subsidized student loan

_____ 18. supply

_____ 19. tuition

_____ 20. value

A. A desired outcome based on one's values for which a plan of action is carried out

B. The quantity of goods and services that producers are willing and able to provide

C. All of the activities related to making and distributing goods and services in a geographic area or country

D. Nontechnical skills needed by most workers for success on the job

E. Describes what a job would be like, including tasks performed and skills needed

F. The willingness and ability of consumers to buy goods and services

G. The alternating periods of growth and decline in the economy

H. Unique skills and abilities that you bring to the job

I. A principle that reflects the worth you place on an idea or action

J. A loan on which interest is not charged until the student graduates

K. The expense paid by students for the instruction at a school

L. A face-to-face meeting with a potential employer to discuss a job opening

M. A gift of money or other aid awarded to a student to help pay for education

N. A set of moral values that people consider acceptable

O. A summary of your work experience, education, skills, and interests that qualify you for a job opening

P. Measurable physical and mental abilities that allow you to complete a job

Q. An employment specialist who seeks out highly qualified people to fill upper-level positions for an employer

R. Spending time observing a worker in a type of job that interests you

S. People who have known you and can provide information about your job skills, character, and achievements

T. A group of friends and acquaintances who keep in contact and share information

EXERCISE 1-2   True/False Questions

Directions: Write the letter "T" for a true statement or "F" for a false statement.

_____ 21. Hard skills are important in getting a job, but soft skills are less important when it comes to keeping a job.

_____ 22. Soft skills can be learned through education and practice.

_____ 23. Job choices you make in your life will not affect your income.

_____ 24. Generally, the higher the education level you achieve, the higher income you can expect to make.

_____ 25. You can stay qualified in a career field with lifelong learning.

_____ 26. Honesty is an example of a value.

_____ 27. Informal education includes things such as self-training and classes you would take at a college.

_____ 28. In a market economy, consumers play a key role in setting prices.

_____ 29. During economic periods of recovery, people slow their buying and are unable to pay high prices.

_____ 30. Scholarships may be available to students with high grades or strong athletic skills.

EXERCISE 1-3   Multiple Choice Questions

Directions: Write the letter of the correct answer in the space provided.

_____ 31. Which of the following is a type of "follow-up" for a job candidate? (a) application letter, (b) thank-you letter, (c) resume, (d) job application

_____ 32. Which of the following should *not* appear on a resume? (a) education, (b) work experience, (c) age, (d) references

_____ 33. Which of the following provides part-time and full-time jobs on a temporary basis? (a) state employment office, (b) headhunter, (c) private employment agency, (d) temp agency

_____ 34. Which of the following is *not* a social networking site? (a) MySpace, (b) JobDango, (c) FaceBook, (d) Twitter

_____ 35. Financial aid that begins charging interest as soon as the loan is granted is called a(n) (a) scholarship, (b) subsidized loan, (c) unsubsidized loan, (d) work-study program

_____ 36. Where can you get advanced training beyond a four-year degree? (a) technical school, (b) graduate program, (c) community college, (d) self-training program

_____ 37. Which of the following is a student organization for business students? (a) FBLA, (b) FFA, (c) PBL, (d) FEA

_____ 38. The stage of the business cycle where the bottom is reached and the economy is at a standstill is called the (a) peak, (b) growth, (c) decline, (d) trough

_____ 39. Which of the following is *not* a type of informal education? (a) on-the-job training, (b) self-training, (c) an Internet language course, (d) a college class

_____ 40. Loyalty is an example of a(n) (a) goal, (b) value, (c) objective, (d) hard skill

EXERCISE 1-4 Building Communications Skills: Listening

Directions: Listen as your teacher or a classmate reads a short passage to you. Use the listening strategies you learned in the textbook. After listening to the passage, complete the sentences below.

1. Nonverbal cues are considered to be very powerful, very _____ forms of communication.

2. Your facial expressions should be friendly, warm, cheerful, and, most important of all, _____.

3. People who genuinely enjoy helping customers exhibit facial expressions that are _____, appropriate, and effective.

4. In situations where a customer has a complaint, friendly yet _____ and sincere facial expressions are most appropriate.

5. Long periods of eye contact may make customers feel _____.

6. Customers may believe the reason you are giving them too little eye contact is because you are trying to _____ or _____ along.

7. When serving a customer, position your body so it _____ the customer.

8. Most businesspeople are most comfortable when they maintain a distance of approximately _____ from another person.

9. Too great a distance between you and customers may prompt both parties to speak _____.

10. Sitting behind a desk creates a _____ that makes conversation less comfortable.

11. One form of touching, a _____, is appropriate in most customer situations.

12. During conversations, avoid _____ that take your focus away from the person to whom you are speaking.

EXERCISE 1-5　Building Math Skills: Computing Pay

Sample Problems

1. Sam's rate of pay is $8.75 per hour. He worked 32 hours last week. Compute his weekly pay.
   Solution: $8.75 × 32 = $280.00

2. Jim makes $800 per month. Compute his yearly salary.
   Solution: $800 × 12 = $9,600 per year

3. Max earns $750 per month. His monthly job hours are 80. Compute his hourly pay.
   Solution: $750/80 = $9.375 = $9.38 per hour

Directions: Complete the problems below. Refer to the sample problems above if needed.

1. Maureen worked 28 hours last week. Her hourly rate is $7.12. What did she earn last week?

2. Carlos worked 40 hours last week. His hourly rate is $9.14. What did he earn last week?

3. Suki's salary is $1,200 per month. What is her yearly salary?

4. Mark's salary is $900 per month. What is his yearly salary?

5. Janet's monthly salary is $1,600. Her monthly job hours are 160. What is her hourly rate of pay?

6. Jim's monthly salary is $1,079.40. His monthly job hours are 140. What is his hourly rate of pay?

EXERCISE 1-6   Careers: Choosing a Job That's Right for You

Directions: In the chart below, circle the job skills or duties that you are interested in exploring. Answer the questions that follow the chart.

Enter data into a computer	Put small pieces together	Draw, using colored pencils or paint	Answer the telephone repeatedly
Stand all day	Move heavy packages onto a cart	Operate a cash register	Remember details of customer orders
Listen carefully to customers' needs	Solve a customer complaint	Help people achieve daily tasks	Talk in front of small groups
Give detailed presentations	Conduct meetings	Prepare written reports	Analyze complicated data
Prepare essay reports	Use heavy equipment	Drive large trucks	Prepare spreadsheets
Build a prototype	Organize projects	Prepare a budget	Hire new employees
Discipline a tardy worker	Compare information to find errors	Solve puzzles	Drive a car as part of your daily job
Make sales presentations	Call people at home	Make decisions that affect lives	Find resources to solve a problem
Work with a large group of people	Work alone in an office	Make decisions that involve large sums of money	Handle cash and account for it
Make products using your hands	Supervise work done by others	Deal effectively with difficult people	Travel extensively to faraway places
Solve math puzzles	Design and present new ideas	Negotiate deals for others	Convince people to make changes
Treat people who are ill or hurt	Counsel people who need advice	Protect others from danger	Rescue people who have been hurt

1. In addition to the skills circled above, what job skills do you have or would you like to learn that are not listed?

2. If you could do anything you wanted for a living, and money was not an issue, what type of career would you choose?

3. If you had a full-time job and wanted another job that you could do for fun, what would that job be?

EXERCISE 1-7   Values and Goals

A value is a principle that reflects the worth you place on an idea or action. The chart below contains sample values and the goals to which they might be related. You may agree with some values, disagree with others, and have additional or different values of your own.

Directions: In the blank chart on the next page, enter several of your values. Then based on those values, list goals (both short-term and long-term) that you think you will want to accomplish in your life.

VALUES	GOALS
Taking care of my health is important.	Develop a physical fitness plan and exercise daily; lose 10 pounds in three months; have yearly medical checkups.
Learning new things is important.	Take a class in chemistry; learn how to key by touch; learn a new software program.
Having close family relationships is important.	Visit my grandmother twice a week; send an e-mail to my cousin in Atlanta once a month.
Having a clean environment is important.	Recycle food and containers; pick up trash; buy materials and products that are less harmful for the environment.
Making and keeping friends is important.	Make a new friend; stay in touch with current friends by visiting or phoning them daily; remember their birthdays; make plans together.
Having financial security is important.	Prepare an education plan that will help achieve the income I need.
Helping others is important.	Volunteer at three local charity groups; donate blood; look for opportunities to be of service.
Maintaining my social network is important.	Join three social networking sites; make positive, informative postings; stay in touch to give and receive good information.
Looking my best is important.	Organize my closet; keep my clothes clean and repaired; replace worn-out clothes; do not choose clothes based on fads.
Enjoying my leisure time is important.	Plan two camping trips a year; buy or borrow equipment to be able to go on long hikes.
Achieving my goals is important.	Work on each goal every week; track my progress.

MY VALUES AND GOALS

VALUES	GOALS

EXERCISE 1-8 Job Description

Directions: Read the job announcement below and then answer the questions that follow.

JOB DESCRIPTION

Job Title

Sales Associate

Job Summary

A sales associate sells merchandise and serves as a retail cashier. This worker assists in restocking, creating displays, and marking prices on merchandise. A positive, friendly attitude is a must for this position.

Salary

$9.00 per hour starting salary

Job Duties

- Provide friendly, courteous, and efficient service to customers
- Answer customers' questions about merchandise and advise customers on merchandise selection
- Record all sales in cash register, receive payment for sales, and issue correct change
- Assist in coding and price marking of merchandise
- Stock shelves, racks, and tables and arrange merchandise displays to attract customers
- Take special orders and handle returns
- Help monitor inventory levels and receive and unpack products
- Keep the store and the stockroom neat and well organized
- Open or close the store and work alone at times
- Attend weekly staff meetings and other meetings as needed
- Perform other related duties as required

Qualifications

- High school diploma required
- Must have worked at least 6 months in a sales position
- Must have a courteous and cooperative attitude
- Must have good reading, math, and communications skills
- Must be able to understand and carry out directions
- Must be honest, dependable, and punctual
- Must be willing to work any day of the week and both day and evening hours
- Must present a clean, neat, and well-groomed appearance
- Must dress in business or business casual attire
- Must be able to lift 40 pounds

1. How much education is required for this job?

2. What hard skills are required for this job? What soft skills are required?

3. Which two of the duties listed do you think are the most important?

4. Which one of the duties listed do you think is the least important?

5. If the employee works 40 hours per week for 50 weeks a year, how much will he or she earn per year at the starting salary listed?

6. Were you surprised to learn of some of the duties required of a sales associate? If so, which duties surprised you?

7. Would this type of work interest you, even as a temporary job to help pay for your education? Why or why not?

EXERCISE 1-9   Must-Ask Questions in a Job Interview

Directions: When you go to a job interview, you will be asked many questions. One of those questions is likely to be, "Do you have any questions for us?" When you are asked this question, you should be prepared to ask good questions—questions that show your interest in the employer and in your own future and questions that provide you with information you might need to know. Below are six questions that you may ask the employer. What kind of information can you gather from the answers to each question?

1.   Is this a newly created position or are you replacing another person? If you are replacing another person, why did he or she leave?

2.   What are your company's long-term (five years or more) plans?

3.   What is the first and most important thing the person doing this job needs to understand?

4.   Can you describe what it is like to work for this company. How would you describe the general work environment?

5.   What can you tell me about the person to whom I would report?

6.   How soon do you expect to hire someone for this position?

EXERCISE 1-10   Networking Notebook

Directions: In Chapter 1, you learned about networking and the value of keeping a list of contacts. To set up or design a networking notebook, consider the types of information about each contact that you might need. For example, if you have an interview or a job opportunity, what types of quick data would you want to have and where or from whom could you get it? Complete the steps below to create a networking notebook.

1.   Get a notebook with several dividers. Label the dividers and start gathering information for each section. You could also create a file in Microsoft® Word or another program to store the information. A formal networking notebook might contain sections with the following labels:

   • Jobs (paid and unpaid)

   • Company name, address, and phone number

   • Supervisor's name, title, and phone number

   • Business contacts (relatives and friends in business)

   • Personal contacts

   • References (current information for several people who would say positive things about you)

   • Letters of reference

2.   Make a to-do list of things you will do to stay in contact with people who can keep you informed and help you with job opportunities.

CHAPTER 2
Income, Benefits, and Taxes

EXERCISE 2-1   Review of Chapter Key Terms

Directions: Write the letter of the correct definition beside its corresponding term.

_____ 1. benefits

_____ 2. commission

_____ 3. disposable income

_____ 4. dividends

_____ 5. entrepreneur

_____ 6. excise taxes

_____ 7. exemption

_____ 8. Form W-2

_____ 9. gross pay

_____ 10. in-cash payments

_____ 11. in-kind payments

_____ 12. Medicare tax

_____ 13. minimum wage

_____ 14. net pay

_____ 15. overtime pay

_____ 16. personal leave

_____ 17. profit-sharing plan

_____ 18. public goods

_____ 19. retirement plan

_____ 20. sales taxes

_____ 21. sick leave

_____ 22. social security tax

_____ 23. transfer payments

_____ 24. unearned income

_____ 25. use taxes

A. Payments made indirectly on a person's behalf or in a form other than money

B. Forms of pay other than salary or wages

C. Government-provided goods and services paid for by taxes

D. A form used to report taxable income a worker received during the calendar year

E. Total salary or wages earned during the pay period

F. A benefit whereby employees may share in the profits of the business

G. Money and benefits received from local, state, or federal governments

H. A tax that pays for medical care for retired persons

I. The amount of your paycheck after deductions

J. A person claimed as a dependent on a tax return

K. Taxes levied on consumer purchases of goods and services

L. Money available to spend or save after taxes have been paid

M. A portion of a corporation's profits distributed to stockholders

N. Paid time away from work due to illness

O. Paid time away from work for personal reasons

P. Taxes based on the use of goods and services provided by the government

Q. Taxes charged on the purchase of specific goods and services

R. Money in the form of check, debit card, or other direct payment given to a person needing assistance

S. A person who takes the risks of being self-employed and owning a business

T. Pay received for hours worked in addition to regular hours

U. An account into which employees contribute a portion of their earnings for their retirement

V. Money received from sources other than working

W. A withholding tax to provide old-age, survivors, and disability insurance

X. Lowest pay rate allowed by law for each hour of work

Y. A set fee or percentage of a sale paid to an employee instead of or in addition to salary or wages

EXERCISE 2-2   True/False Questions

Directions: Write the letter "T" for a true statement or "F" for a false statement.

_____ 26.   Self-employment income is a form of unearned income.
_____ 27.   All states have the same minimum wage rate.
_____ 28.   Overtime is generally 1 ½ times the regular rate of pay.
_____ 29.   Tips are not subject to federal or state income tax.
_____ 30.   Commission income is earned only when a sale is made.
_____ 31.   An entrepreneur is a person who owns his or her own business.
_____ 32.   Owning a business is usually considered less risky than working as an employee.
_____ 33.   A lifestyle business is one that will not go on to become a publicly held corporation.
_____ 34.   People whose parents own a business are more likely to start a business than people
              whose parents are employees.
_____ 35.   A business plan clearly describes the steps that will be taken to open and operate a
              business.
_____ 36.   Most benefits received by employees are not taxable.
_____ 37.   Disposable income refers to the amount of money a worker has to spend or save.
_____ 38.   Pay without work includes vacations, holidays, and sick pay.
_____ 39.   Employer-provided health insurance is considered a perk for employees.
_____ 40.   Group life insurance is usually more expensive than an individual policy.

EXERCISE 2-3   Multiple Choice Questions

Directions: Write the letter of the correct answer in the space provided.

_____ 41.   Which of the following is a retirement plan in which employees set aside pretax
              earnings? (a) profit-sharing plan, (b) 401(k), (c) Flex 125, (d) HSA
_____ 42.   Which of the following is a form of unearned income? (a) wages, (b) salaries,
              (c) interest earnings, (d) tips
_____ 43.   Which of the following is an example of variable income? (a) interest earnings,
              (b) dividends, (c) commisions, (d) rent
_____ 44.   Which of the following is an in-cash transfer payment? (a) unemployment
              compensation, (b) food stamps, (c) rent subsidies, (d) vouchers
_____ 45.   Which of the following is considered an "entitlement" program? (a) unemployment
              compensation, (b) social security, (c) workers' compensation, (d) veterans' benefits
_____ 46.   Which of the following is considered a "use" tax? (a) gasoline tax, (b) sales tax,
              (c) income tax, (d) property tax
_____ 47.   Income taxes are an example of which kind of tax? (a) regressive, (b) proportional,
              (c) progressive, (d) ad valorem
_____ 48.   An inheritance tax is an example of which kind of tax? (a) income tax, (b) sales tax,
              (c) wealth tax, (d) luxury tax
_____ 49.   Which of the following forms is used to verify eligibility to work in the United States?
              (a) Form W-2, (b) Form I-9, (c) Form W-4, (d) Form 1099
_____ 50.   Which of the following is *not* a public good? (a) roads, (b) public education,
              (c) national parks, (d) church buildings

EXERCISE 2-4 Building Communications Skills: Critical Listening

Directions: Listen as your teacher or a classmate reads a short passage to you. After listening to the passage, answer the questions below.

1. List the four factors of production.

2. List the payoff or payback for each of the four factors of production.

3. How is a capitalistic society different from a socialistic or a communistic society in terms of what is produced and what an individual can choose to buy?

4. What is productivity? What can cause it to increase?

5. What is meant by investing or investment?

6. Why does a business owner need to make a profit?

7. List two questions you would ask about the factors of production and an individual's ability to have income from all four.

7. Duc works for a salary of $2,200 per month. His computed hourly rate of pay is $13.75 per hour. Although Duc earns a salary, he sometimes qualifies for overtime pay for special situations. For overtime hours, he earns 1½ times his regular computed hourly rate. Last month, he worked for 14 paid overtime hours. He has federal income tax withheld at the rate of 15%, social security tax at the rate of 6.2%, Medicare tax at the rate of 1.45%, and health insurance premiums of $85 per month. What was his net pay?

8. Janice works for a salary of $2,396 per month. She has federal income tax withheld at the rate of 15%, social security tax at the rate of 6.2%, Medicare tax at the rate of 1.45%, and health insurance premiums of $95 per month. What is her net pay?

9. Zurab works for a salary of $1,986 per month. He has federal income tax withheld at the rate of 15%, social security tax at the rate of 6.2%, Medicare tax at the rate of 1.45%, and health insurance premiums of $48 per month. Zurab also contributes to a savings plan. Each month, 2% of his gross pay is placed in the plan. Zurab pays income tax on this money. What is his net pay?

EXERCISE 2-6   Careers: Is Self-Employment Right for You?

Directions: For each statement below, circle 0 if you do not agree with the statement at all. Circle 3 if you agree somewhat (or some of the time), and circle 5 if you absolutely agree. These statements and ratings describe you or your beliefs, values, or attributes. When you have finished, compute your score, and evaluate it using the scale on the next page.

1.	I like to set the pace, work alone, and make the rules.	0	3	5
2.	I work hard at achieving my goals.	0	3	5
3.	When I start a project, I keep working until it is finished —no matter how long it takes.	0	3	5
4.	I like to get up early and get going.	0	3	5
5.	I like to play competitive games like MONOPOLY® or Risk.	0	3	5
6.	I take good care of myself and have high expectations of myself.	0	3	5
7.	I have strong willpower; I get things done.	0	3	5
8.	My friends would say that I am a self-starter and a go-getter.	0	3	5
9.	My friends would say that I am responsible.	0	3	5
10.	My friends would say that I have good people skills.	0	3	5
11.	I am good at keeping track of expenses; I save money and plan ahead.	0	3	5
12.	I am organized and focused.	0	3	5
13.	I am independent and like being on my own.	0	3	5
14.	I don't mind sacrificing now for security in the future.	0	3	5
15.	I am outgoing and able to deal with the public.	0	3	5
16.	I am a leader; I like telling others what to do and following up to be sure they did it.	0	3	5
17.	My parents or other close family members own their own business or are self-employed.	0	3	5
18.	I don't like being told what to do, when to do it, or how to do it.	0	3	5
19.	I don't want to be limited in my personal growth or income potential.	0	3	5
20.	I don't feel anxious when I'm on my own; I like finding things to do.	0	3	5

A. Scoring

Add up your points. What is your score? _____

Use this scale to assess your score:

- If your score is 0–50 points, you probably should be an employee and work in a traditional career. The risks of self-employment probably would outweigh the benefits for you.

- If your score is 51–75 points, you could work for others or have your own small business or both. You might try starting a small side business and see whether it does well and whether you like it.

- If your score is more than 75 points, you should strongly consider going into business for yourself. The higher the score, the more likely you are to enjoy being an entrepreneur.

B. Your Interests and Skills

Answer these questions:

1. What are your hobbies? (What do you like to do in your spare time?)

2. If you had enough time and resources, what would you like to learn to do well?

3. Do you have a particular skill or aptitude; for example, can you do or make something that others would buy?

EXERCISE 2-7   Workplace Ethics

Directions: Read the following descriptions of workplace situations. Think about or discuss with others the ethical dilemmas that arise from them. Then decide how you would resolve each situation. Think of questions you would ask and factors to consider other than the information given. What factors would influence or change your decision? Write your response to each situation under the situation description.

Situation 1

Robert has been working at Miller Enterprises for several years. Last week, you saw Robert falsify his time card. He punched in but did not work that day. His friend Erin punched out for him. When you asked Robert where he was, he said that he had to go to the dentist. He told you that he doesn't want to use sick leave or personal leave for dental appointments but that he always works extra hours to make up the time. Robert is not your supervisor. He works in a different department. However, he provides a service to the department where you work. When he was absent, your department was delayed in submitting a report because he wasn't there.

Situation 2

Racine works in customer service. She talks to customers and resolves disputes. Racine often has to deal with angry and frustrated people. Sometimes they want to return or exchange goods but do not have the proper receipts. Recently a customer brought back a dress that had obviously been worn. It had stains on it. The customer insisted that the dress was that way when she purchased it. She had a receipt for the purchase of the dress a week ago.

Situation 3

Company policy allows for 10 days of sick leave and 4 days of personal leave a year. Employees get 10 days of vacation a year for the first 5 years, 20 days a year for the next 5 years, and 30 days a year after 10 years. Sick leave accumulates for up to 100 days. Kathy's employment record shows that each year she takes all the personal leave, vacation days, and sick leave to which she is entitled. Even when Kathy is not sick, she calls in sick to be sure she uses all her sick leave each year. When a friend asks about the amount of time Kathy takes off, Kathy says, "It's my benefit, and I take full advantage of it. I don't want to leave any unused pay without work on the table."

Situation 4

Joaquim is a new employee. His shift begins at 8 a.m. Joaquim's supervisor is often late, arriving after 9 a.m. Most of the other workers also arrive late or cover for those who are late. Customer service is often not sufficient during the first hour of business. The manager is aware of customer complaints of poor service but is unaware of the tardiness problem, since she does not arrive until later. What should Joaquim do?

Situation 5

Martin works at a restaurant. Part of his benefits package is a free dinner if he works from 4 to 7 p.m. Martin's shift usually does not start until after 7 p.m., but he arrives early to eat dinner. Martin also snacks on restaurant food during his shift. On his break, he eats a late meal. Martin says that eating at the restaurant is one of the perks of his job. Other employees have started doing the same thing.

EXERCISE 2-8   Tax Form 1040EZ

Directions:

1. Access **www.cengage.com/school/pfinance/pfl** and click on the link for Chapter 2. Open and print the data file *CH02 Form 1040EZ*.

2. Shown below is a Form W-2. Based on the Form W-2, prepare a 1040EZ tax return, computing tax due or a refund. Use the tax tables in the data file *2009 Partial Tax Tables*. The taxpayer is filing a single return. There is no interest income. Sign the form using the name **Lisle Garner**. Use **Cashier** for the occupation and **703-555-0134** for the phone number.

a Employee's social security number 000 22 2106	OMB No. 1545-0008	Safe, accurate, FAST! Use	IRS e-file	Visit the IRS website at www.irs.gov/efile.

b Employer identification number (EIN) 00-000000	1 Wages, tips, other compensation $18,916.00	2 Federal income tax withheld $1,920.00

c Employer's name, address, and ZIP code Jerry's Food Stores 4842 West Hanover Drive Reston, VA 20190-4842	3 Social security wages $18,916.00	4 Social security tax withheld $1,172.79
	5 Medicare wages and tips $18,916.00	6 Medicare tax withheld $274.28
	7 Social security tips	8 Allocated tips

d Control number	9 Advance EIC payment	10 Dependent care benefits

e Employee's first name and initial Last name Suff.	11 Nonqualified plans	12a See instructions for box 12
Lisle Garner 48 West Place, Apt. 11 Reston, VA 20194-0048	13 Statutory employee □ Retirement plan □ Third-party sick pay □	12b
	14 Other	12c
		12d
f Employee's address and ZIP code		

15 State VA	Employer's state ID number 00000	16 State wages, tips, etc. $18,916.00	17 State income tax $224.30	18 Local wages, tips, etc. $18,916.00	19 Local income tax 0	20 Locality name Reston

Form **W-2** **Wage and Tax Statement**   **2009**   Department of the Treasury—Internal Revenue Service

Copy B—To Be Filed With Employee's FEDERAL Tax Return.
This information is being furnished to the Internal Revenue Service.

EXERCISE 2-9   Tax Form 1040EZ

Directions:

1.   Access **www.cengage.com/school/pfinance/pfl** and click on the link for Chapter 2. Open and print the data file *CH02 Form 1040EZ*.

2.   Shown below is a Form W-2. Based on the Form W-2, prepare a 1040EZ tax return, computing the tax due or a refund. Use the tax tables in the data file *2009 Partial Tax Tables*. The taxpayer is filing a single return. There is no interest income. Sign the form using the name **Enrique Mendez**. Use **Sales Associate** for the occupation and **972-555-0156** for the phone number.

a Employee's social security number 000 22 2107		Safe, accurate, FAST! Use IRS e-file	Visit the IRS website at www.irs.gov/efile
b Employer identification number (EIN) 00-000000	**1** Wages, tips, other compensation $26,411.00	**2** Federal income tax withheld $2,300.00
c Employer's name, address, and ZIP code	**3** Social security wages $26,411.00	**4** Social security tax withheld $1,637.48
Miller's Department Store 23 Westlake Drive Dallas, TX 75202-5226	**5** Medicare wages and tips $26,411.00	**6** Medicare tax withheld 382.96
	7 Social security tips	**8** Allocated tips
d Control number	**9** Advance EIC payment	**10** Dependent care benefits
e Employee's first name and initial Last name Suff.	**11** Nonqualified plans	**12a** See instructions for box 12
Enrique Mendez 276 Prairie Road Dallas, TX 75201-0276	**13** Statutory employee ☐ Retirement plan ☐ Third-party sick pay ☐	**12b**
	14 Other	**12c**
		12d
f Employee's address and ZIP code		

15 State TX	Employer's state ID number 00000	16 State wages, tips, etc. $26,411.00	17 State income tax $311.40	18 Local wages, tips, etc. $26,411.00	19 Local income tax 0	20 Locality name Dallas

Form **W-2** Wage and Tax Statement   **2009**   Department of the Treasury—Internal Revenue Service

Copy B—To Be Filed With Employee's FEDERAL Tax Return.
This information is being furnished to the Internal Revenue Service.

CHAPTER 3
Your Purchasing Power

EXERCISE 3-1   Review of Chapter Key Terms

Directions: Write the letter of the correct definition beside its corresponding term.

_____ 1.   advertising

_____ 2.   branding strategy

_____ 3.   cost-plus pricing

_____ 4.   cost-push inflation

_____ 5.   deception

_____ 6.   deflation

_____ 7.   demand-pull inflation

_____ 8.   direct advertising

_____ 9.   disinflation

_____ 10. economizing

_____ 11. hyperinflation

_____ 12. inflation

_____ 13. low-balling

_____ 14. market-based pricing

_____ 15. markup

_____ 16. normal profit

_____ 17. optimizing

_____ 18. pop-up ads

_____ 19. rational buying

_____ 20. real-cost inflation

_____ 21. space-shifting

_____ 22. target audience

_____ 23. time-shifting

_____ 24. time value of money

_____ 25. value-based pricing

A. Rapidly rising prices that are out of control

B. Rising prices as a result of rising production costs

C. The percentage amount added to production cost to obtain the price of an item

D. Setting a price based on production costs plus markup

E. Internet ads that open a new window that pops onto the screen in front of the web page being viewed

F. Setting prices to be competitive with prices of similar products currently being sold

G. Advertising a basic service at an unusually low price and then claiming additional repairs or services are needed

H. Setting a price based on how much consumers will pay

I. Increase in the general level of prices

J. A concept that says a dollar you receive in the future will be worth less than a dollar you receive today

K. Copying content from one form of media to another

L. Saving as much as possible and spending money only when necessary

M. Rising prices due to scarce resources or increased difficulty in obtaining resources

N. Informing consumers about products and encouraging them to buy

O. Decrease in the general level of prices

P. Recording video or audio for later viewing or listening

Q. False or misleading claims made about the quality, price, or purpose of a product

R. Higher prices as a result of consumers wanting to buy more goods and services than producers supply

S. Process of selecting goods and services based on need, want, and logical choices

T. Getting the highest value for the money spent

U. A specific group of people who are likely to buy a product

V. A profit that allows a business to survive and grow

W. Rising prices with the rate of increase slowing down

X. Distribution of product information directly to consumers

Y. Carrying well-known brand names to attract customers who are loyal to those brands

Directions: Write the letter "T" for a true statement or "F" for a false statement.

_____ **26.** The economy changes with the habits and attitudes of producers and consumers.

_____ **27.** A cost-of-living raise (COLA) will give the consumer more purchasing power.

_____ **28.** Hyperinflation has not occurred in the United States except for rapidly increasing food prices.

_____ **29.** The monetary policy refers to the actions taken by the Federal Reserve System (Fed) to help stabilize the economy.

_____ **30.** Inflation increases your purchasing power.

_____ **31.** With optimizing, you are saving as much as possible and spending money only when necessary.

_____ **32.** Advertising is a method of creating demand to promote sales.

_____ **33.** Customer loyalty programs are a form of direct advertising where the message goes directly to the consumer.

_____ **34.** The FDA approves the sale of foods, drugs, cosmetics, and medical devices.

_____ **35.** Clearance and liquidation are sales techniques that involve slashing prices drastically.

EXERCISE 3-3   Multiple Choice Questions

Directions: Write the letter of the correct answer in the space provided.

_____ **36.** Which of the following occurs when high prices are lowered due to decreased demand, but then are restored to the previous high level? (a) disinflation, (b) reflation, (c) hyperinflation, (d) deflation

_____ **37.** Which form of inflation is created by consumers spending money too fast? (a) cost-push, (b) demand-pull, (c) real-cost, (d) productivity

_____ **38.** Double-digit inflation is known as (a) disinflation, (b) reflation, (c) hyperinflation, (d) deflation

_____ **39.** Which of the following pricing strategies is most likely to be used for a new technology product that incurred high research and development costs? (a) cost-recovery, (b) value-based, (c) cost-plus, (d) market-based

_____ **40.** Which of the following occurs when people buy products based on desire rather than logic? (a) rational buying, (b) emotional buying, (c) impulse buying, (d) economizing

_____ **41.** Which of the following federal agencies regulates false and deceptive advertising? (a) USDA, (b) FDA, (c) FTC, (d) SEC

_____ **42.** Which of the following schemes is an illegal multilevel marketing gimmick? (a) bait and switch, (b) pyramid schemes, (c) fake sales, (d) pigeon drop

_____ **43.** Which of the following scheme occurs when an expert investor promises very high returns and then steals the money? (a) fake sales, (b) pyramid schemes, (c) ponzi schemes, (d) pigeon drop

_____ **44.** Which of the following does inflation affect? (a) employment, (b) saving, (c) investing, (d) all of the above

_____ **45.** When people buy on the spur of the moment, it is called (a) rational buying, (b) emotional buying, (c) impulse buying, (d) wise buying

EXERCISE 3-4   Building Communications Skills: Creative Listening

Directions: Listen as your teacher or a classmate reads a short passage to you. After listening to the passage, answer the questions below.

1. Who gets hurt the most by inflation? Describe a typical person in this position.

2. Who is able to adjust to rising prices? Give some examples of why.

3. Who benefits from inflation? Describe a person who is in this position.

4. What are some things you can do to avoid getting hurt by inflation?

5. What additional questions do you have about rising prices and how to cope with them?

EXERCISE 3-5   Building Math Skills: Computing Unit Prices

Directions: Using the information given below, compute unit prices. Express the answers in dollars and cents. Round up to the nearest penny when the third decimal number is 5 or higher. Round down to the nearest penny when the third decimal number is 4 or lower.

1. 6 for $1.00

2. 3 for $1.99

3. 15 ounces for $2.49

4. $6.49 for 36 ounces

5. $5.99 for a box of 24

6. 2 for 79 cents

7. $8.99 for a 12-oz. box

8. $1.06 for a 22-oz. bottle

9. 10 for $2.99

10. 12 for $1.00

11. $13.00 for a case of 24

12. $2.99 for a 32-ounce jar

13. $4.95 for a carton of 6

14. $24.99 for 10 bottles

EXERCISE 3-6   Sales Careers

There are many types of careers in sales, from counter help at a retail store to full-commission sales in a new car dealership. People who are successful in sales have the following traits and skills:

- Outgoing
- Energetic
- Resourceful
- Creative
- Self-confident
- Friendly

- Good communicator
- Persistent
- Sensible
- Logical
- Strong leadership skills
- Good problem solver

Directions: Answer the following questions to explore a career in sales.

1.   Which of the traits and skills listed above do you have?

2.   Is a career in sales something that interests you?

3.   List several types of sales jobs. Which ones do you find most appealing? Least appealing?

4.   Give the name and position (type of sales) of someone you know who is currently working in sales. Ask this person the following questions: "What do you like best about selling products? What do you like least?" Record the person's responses.

EXERCISE 3-7   Customer Service

Directions: Read the following scenarios. For each one, list ways that customer service could be improved and the shopping experience made more pleasant for the customer.

Scenario 1

Deisiane and her mother were shopping for a new pair of shoes for Deisiane. The store was crowded, and many people were waiting to be served. Deisiane had chosen three pairs of shoes to try on. She and her mother were sitting in the designated area for trying on shoes. After about five minutes, another person also sat down to wait. There were many more customers than sales associates, and soon two more people were seated. A hurried salesclerk came over and apologized for the delay. He assured the customers that they would be assisted shortly. After ten more minutes, one of the salesclerks rushed over and helped the customer who was seated after Deisiane. Then another associate helped another person who also had arrived after Deisiane. Feeling slighted and frustrated, Deisiane and her mother left the store.

Scenario 2

Devon, a sales associate, was working late helping a customer finish her purchase. The customer had a lot of questions. Devon tried to answer those questions as best as he could, but he had only been working in the home goods department for two days. He called a coworker to help him. While he was waiting for the coworker to arrive, Devon answered a phone call. The call was about a product, but the customer in the store was upset because she felt ignored. After 15 minutes, the customer threw up her hands and left the store.

EXERCISE 3-9 Advertising

Directions: Think about a product that you recently purchased or would like to purchase. Assume you are the manufacturer or business that is selling the product. How would you create demand for the product through advertising? Answer the following questions to determine what types of advertising you would use.

1. What is your product? Who is your target audience? Describe the characteristics of your target audience.

2. What form of advertising do you think would work the best—newspaper, magazine, television, radio, Internet, or billboards and signs? Explain your answer.

3. Can you use direct advertising for this product? Why or why not?

4. Is it possible to create demand for the product by using a customer loyalty program? If so, describe how the program would work.

5. Assume you are going to advertise the product on the radio. Write a script for the ad describing the product's features and benefits. You may also want to write a jingle for the product to help consumers remember it.

CHAPTER 4
Financial Decisions and Planning

EXERCISE 4-1   Review of Chapter Key Terms

Directions: Write the letter of the correct definition beside its corresponding term.

_____ 1. assets

_____ 2. benchmarks

_____ 3. budget

_____ 4. cash inflows

_____ 5. cash outflows

_____ 6. charitable giving

_____ 7. electronic records

_____ 8. encryption

_____ 9. financial goals

_____ 10. financial plan

_____ 11. financial planner

_____ 12. financial resources

_____ 13. fixed expenses

_____ 14. identity theft

_____ 15. liabilities

_____ 16. needs

_____ 17. net worth

_____ 18. opportunity cost

_____ 19. personal goals

_____ 20. phishing

_____ 21. timeline

_____ 22. tradeoff

_____ 23. variable expenses

_____ 24. variances

_____ 25. wants

A. The value of your next best option—what you are giving up

B. Money or other items of value that are used to acquire goods and services

C. Costs that can go up and down each month

D. Debts that you owe

E. A scam in which an e-mail is sent from someone posing as your bank or other legitimate business asking for personal information

F. Process of converting data to a coded form

G. Costs that do not change each month

H. Donating money or time to a cause in which you believe

I. A visual display of how long it will take to achieve each phase of a plan

J. Differences between planned amounts and actual amounts

K. Plans for how you will pay for your personal goals

L. Expenses, or items for which you must spend money

M. A spending and saving plan based on expected income and expenses

N. Things people desire for reasons beyond survival and basic comfort

O. A professional consultant who provides financial advice for a fee or commission

P. The use of your personal information by someone else to commit fraud or other crimes

Q. Giving up one option in exchange for another

R. Things you want to achieve in your life

S. Income from your job, investments, and other sources

T. The difference between assets and liabilities

U. Money and items of value that you own

V. Soft-copy formats of your financial information stored on your computer

W. A comprehensive plan listing goals along with steps and a timeline for reaching them

X. Standards against which progress is measured

Y. Things needed for survival, such as food, clothing, and shelter

Directions: Write the letter "T" for a true statement or "F" for a false statement.

_____ 26.   People who do not have their basic needs met are not able to provide for other needs or wants.

_____ 27.   Basic needs are those needs that allow you to have a comfortable lifestyle.

_____ 28.   Financial resources are unlimited and growing.

_____ 29.   The amount of money a person has to spend after needs are met is called discretionary income.

_____ 30.   Wealth is measured on the personal net worth statement.

_____ 31.   One way to increase wealth is to spend less than you make.

_____ 32.   A personal net worth statement lists income and expenses.

_____ 33.   A tradeoff is the value of what you are giving up when you make a purchase.

_____ 34.   Receiving a pay raise will allow you to increase your discretionary income.

_____ 35.   You can build your vocabulary by reading.

_____ 36.   Microsoft Word is an example of a spreadsheet program.

_____ 37.   Balancing your budget is a simple six-step process.

_____ 38.   Charitable giving is a mandatory fixed expense.

_____ 39.   A favorable variance results from spending less than you budgeted for spending.

_____ 40.   Keeping good records will help you prepare a better budget.

Directions: Write the letter of the correct answer in the space provided.

_____ 41.   For each pesonal goal you should have a(n) ____ goal. (a) timeline, (b) benchmark, (c) financial, (d) expert

_____ 42.   Which of the following is *not* a financial record? (a) personal budget (b) checkbook, (c) tax return, (d) all of the above are financial records

_____ 43.   A goal that you want to achieve in three to four years is a(n) (a) short-term goal, (b) medium-term goal, (c) long-term goal, (d) timeline

_____ 44.   Financial plans (a) change over time, (b) do not change over time, (c) require a short-term commitment, (d) do not reflect your values over time

_____ 45.   Which of the following financial professionals is likely to publish self-help materials? (a) financial planner, (b) financial adviser, (c) financial expert, (d) investment adviser

_____ 46.   Which of the following can help protect your computer from hackers? (a) firewall, (b) passwords, (c) encryption, (d) all of the above

_____ 47.   Which of the following is a luxury item? (a) food, (b) medical care, (c) more than one pair of shoes, (d) sports car

_____ 48.   Which of the following is *not* listed on a personal net worth statement? (a) income, (b) assets, (c) liabilities, (d) net worth

_____ 49.   Which of the following is a fixed expense? (a) food, (b) rent, (c) entertainment, (d) utilities

_____ 50.   Which of the following is a variable expense? (a) rent, (b) food, (c) insurance, (d) car payment

EXERCISE 4-4   Building Communications Skills: Reading Vocabulary

Directions: Improve your vocabulary by learning the meanings of the following terms related to personal finance. For each term, consult a dictionary or another source to find the meaning. Some terms can be found in the glossary of your textbook. Write the meaning for each term. Then write a sentence that uses the term and shows its meaning.

1.   **capital gain**

2.   **compound interest**

3.   **estate**

4.   **itinerary**

5.   **monopoly**

6. overdraft

7. power of attorney

8. rebate

9. tenant

10. usury

EXERCISE 4-5   Building Math Skills: Computing Variances

Directions: For the amounts below, compute the variances in dollar amounts and in percentages. Round to the nearest whole percent. Indicate whether the variance is favorable (F) or unfavorable (U).

Budgeted Amount	Actual Amount	Dollar Variance	Percent Variance	F or U
Income Amounts				
1. $500.00	$400.00	_____	_____	_____
2. $25.00	$17.50	_____	_____	_____
3. $150.00	$120.00	_____	_____	_____
4. $300.00	$325.00	_____	_____	_____
5. $225.00	$250.00	_____	_____	_____
6. $50.00	$75.00	_____	_____	_____
Expense Amounts				
7. $255.00	$225.00	_____	_____	_____
8. $106.00	$100.00	_____	_____	_____
9. $52.00	$66.00	_____	_____	_____
10. $35.00	$25.00	_____	_____	_____
11. $215.00	$200.00	_____	_____	_____
12. $300.00	$150.00	_____	_____	_____

EXERCISE 4-6   Budgeting

Directions: Below is Alex's budget for January. He just learned that his work hours have been reduced. He will earn $100 less in January than he planned, or a monthly total of $300. Complete the steps below.

1.   Recreate the budget for Alex Perez. Use spreadsheet software, if available. If spreadsheet software is not available, record the budget on paper.

2.   Based on what you have learned about fixed and variable expenses, revise the budget so it balances at the new estimated income level. Explain why you chose to change the items you did to make the budget balance.

ALEX PEREZ
BUDGET FOR JANUARY 20—

	Weekly	Monthly
Income		
Allowance	$25.00	$100.00
Part-time job earnings	100.00	400.00
Total income	$125.00	$500.00
Savings	$12.50	$50.00
Expenses		
Loan payment	$50.00	$200.00
Entertainment	30.00	120.00
Food for lunches	25.00	100.00
Miscellaneous	7.50	30.00
Total expenses	$112.50	$450.00
Total expenses and savings	$125.00	$500.00

EXERCISE 4-7   Financial Plan

Directions: Personal financial planning begins with setting goals. What personal goals do you want to achieve. What financial goals do you think you will need to set to achieve these goals? What benchmarks should you set? What timeline do you think will be needed? Complete the table with personal goals, financial goals, benchmarks, and timelines.

PERSONAL GOALS	FINANCIAL GOALS	BENCHMARKS	TIMELINE

EXERCISE 4-8   Internet Research

Many people use the Internet to do research, from reading about a new medical breakthrough to finding a plumber. One valuable type of research is product and price comparisons. You can search for services and products and compare their features and prices. This saves you both time and money.

Internet search engines, such as Google and Yahoo!, enable you to enter keywords to find all types of information. This includes historical facts and data, as well as current events. Keywords should be nouns—persons, places, or things—that are likely to be found on the web pages you want to view. When the search is complete, a list of links, also called hits, will appear. Clicking on a link will take you to a web page containing information related to the keywords.

Directions: Using the following keywords, find and visit several links. Write a sentence describing what you found at each link.

1.   Budgets

2.   Recordkeeping

3.   Financial advice

4.   Consumer frauds

5.   Firewall

EXERCISE 4-9   Personal Financial Statements

Directions: Identifying the income, expenses, assets, and liabilities you have now is a good place to begin planning for your financial future. Create a personal cash flow statement, personal net worth statement, and budget following the steps below.

1. Review the personal cash flow statement shown in Figure 4-1.1 of your textbook. Create a similar statement using your information. Use spreadsheet software, if available, to create the statement.

    a. List all your cash inflows—money you receive from any source during one month.

    b. List all your cash outflows—money you pay for goods and services or other expenses during the same month.

    c. Find the total of your cash inflows and the total of your cash outflows. Subtract the cash outflows from the cash inflows to find your net cash flow.

2. Review the personal net worth statement shown in Figure 4-1.2 of your textbook. Create a similar statement using your information. Use spreadsheet software, if available, to create the statement.

    a. List all your assets—money you have or things of value you own.

    b. List all your liabilities—debts you owe that must be repaid.

    c. Subtract liabilities from assets to compute your net worth.

3. Review the personal budget shown in Figure 4-2.2 of your textbook. Create a similar budget using your personal information. Use spreadsheet software, if available, to create the budget.

    a. Estimate your income—earned or unearned on a monthly and yearly basis.

    b. Plan your savings—estimate the amount you can set aside each month and year.

    c. Estimate your expenses—both variable and fixed. Include charitable giving if you wish.

    d. Balance the budget.

    e. Can you improve your budget? If so, how?

CHAPTER 5
The Banking System

EXERCISE 5-1   Review of Chapter Key Terms

Directions: Write the letter of the correct definition beside its corresponding term.

_____ 1. annuity

_____ 2. bounced check

_____ 3. cashier's check

_____ 4. certificate of deposit

_____ 5. check

_____ 6. checkbook register

_____ 7. checking account

_____ 8. compound interest

_____ 9. debit card

_____ 10. deposit

_____ 11. endorsement

_____ 12. floating a check

_____ 13. inactive account

_____ 14. Internet banking

_____ 15. money market account

_____ 16. money order

_____ 17. postdated check

_____ 18. principal

_____ 19. Rule of 72

_____ 20. savings account

_____ 21. simple interest

_____ 22. smart card

_____ 23. stop payment

_____ 24. U.S. savings bond

_____ 25. withdrawal

A. A card used to withdraw or deduct money from your checking account

B. A tool used to track checking account transactions

C. A fixed amount set aside on a regular basis over time

D. An instruction to the bank not to honor a check that has been issued or lost

E. Interest earned on both principal and previously earned interest

F. Money added to a checking or savings account

G. A check used to pay bills for which money is guaranteed

H. A check issued against the bank's funds

I. A quick formula for computing how long it will take to double money invested at a given interest rate

J. A card that contains a computer chip that stores electronic money

K. A discount bond issued by the federal government

L. A type of savings account that earns the market rate of interest on the money deposited

M. A time deposit that pays a fixed rate of interest for a specified length of time

N. Accessing and managing your account online

O. Interest computed on principal once during a certain time period

P. A check that is returned to the payee's bank due to nonsufficient funds

Q. Writing a check and planning to make a deposit later to cover it before the check is processed

R. A demand deposit in a bank on which checks are drawn

S. A demand deposit account designed for the accumulation of money in a safe place for future use

T. A check written with a date that will occur in the future

U. A written order to a bank to pay a stated amount to a person

V. A sum of money set aside on which interest is paid

W. Taking money from your account

X. A signature on the back of a check

Y. An account that does not meet minimum usage requirements

EXERCISE 5-2   True/False Questions

Directions: Write the letter "T" for a true statement or "F" for a false statement.

_____ **26.** Most people do not keep a checking account because it is too much trouble.
_____ **27.** A checking account allows easy access (liquidity) to the cash in your account.
_____ **28.** A canceled check serves as proof of payment for bills or purchases.
_____ **29.** Most checking accounts have some type of fee unless certain conditions are met.
_____ **30.** With online banking it is not necessary to reconcile your account or to verify your balance.
_____ **31.** Checks should be written in ink with all spaces filled in.
_____ **32.** The payee is the person who is writing the check.
_____ **33.** Debit cards can be used for ATM transactions but not to make purchases.
_____ **34.** If a check is not properly endorsed, it may be returned by the bank to the customer and not deposited.
_____ **35.** You should reconcile your bank statements once a year.
_____ **36.** A third-party check can easily be cashed or deposited into any account.
_____ **37.** When a check is converted to a digital image, the check is truncated (not returned to you).
_____ **38.** Savings accounts are insured by the FDIC the same as checking accounts.

EXERCISE 5-3   Multiple Choice Questions

Directions: Write the letter of the correct answer in the space provided.

_____ **39.** Interest paid only on the principal is called (a) interest expense, (b) simple interest, (c) compound interest, (d) imputed interest
_____ **40.** If you set aside $1,000 for one year at 6% simple interest, how much interest will you earn at the end of one year? (a) $6.00, (b) $60.00, (c) $600.00, (d) $0.60
_____ **41.** Which of the following endorsements would include the instructions "for deposit only"? (a) blank, (b) full, (c) restrictive, (d) special
_____ **42.** Using the Rule of 72, if you can invest your money at 10%, how long will it take to double your investment amount? (a) 5 years, (b) 6 years, (c) 7.2 years, (d) 8.5 years
_____ **43.** Which of the following would *not* be kept in a safe deposit box? (a) driver's license, (b) will, (c) insurance policy, (d) deed
_____ **44.** Which of the following is issued by a bank against its own funds? (a) third-party check, (b) money order, (c) stop payment, (d) cashier's check
_____ **45.** Which of the following banking activities cannot be done on the Internet? (a) paying bills, (b) withdrawing cash, (c) monitoring accounts, (d) transferring money
_____ **46.** Overdraft protection helps you avoid (a) ATM fees, (b) inactive account fees, (c) monthly service fees, (d) nonsufficient fund fees
_____ **47.** All of the following may be required to open a checking account *except* a (a) security question, (b) signature card, (c) cashier's check, (d) minimum deposit
_____ **48.** An account with two or more people is called a (a) special account, (b) joint account, (c) signature account, (d) free account

EXERCISE 5-4   Building Communications Skills: Reading Comprehension

Directions: Read the following passage in order to learn and remember the information presented. Underline or highlight key words. Focus on the main purpose of each paragraph. Read the passage again, focusing on details and vocabulary. Then answer the questions that follow the passage.

The Fed buys and sells U.S. Treasury securities. When you buy one of these securities, you are lending money to the U.S. government. There are many types of U.S. securities, ranging from short-term bills to long-term bonds. All of them are very safe choices for the saver who wants to set aside money with little or no risk. U.S. Treasury securities can be purchased electronically. You will receive an electronic confirmation that is proof of purchase. They are not subject to state or local income tax. All securities are subject to federal income tax, except for EE Bonds and I Bonds bought for education purposes.

Treasury bills, called T-bills, are sold for terms ranging from a 4 to 52 weeks. They are sold at a discount from face value. For example, you might pay $950 for a $1,000 T-bill. When the bill matures, you are paid the face value of $1,000. The difference between the purchase price ($950) and the maturity value ($1,000) is called interest. Remember, the time between purchase and sale is very short—52 weeks or less. The discount rate is determined at auction. The minimum purchase is $100, and you can buy in multiples of $100. You can also buy T-bills through banks and brokers. You can hold a bill until it matures, or you can sell it before it matures.

Treasury notes, called T-notes, pay a fixed rate of interest every 6 months until maturity. They are issued for terms of 2, 3, 5, 7, and 10 years. The rate earned on T-notes is set when the notes are auctioned. The minimum purchase is $100, and they are sold in multiples of $100. T-notes may also be sold at a discount, at face value, or at greater than face value. At maturity, the face value of the note is paid to the owner.

Treasury bonds are auctioned in February, May, August, and November. They pay interest every 6 months for 30 years. The minimum purchase is $100. Treasury bonds may be sold at any time.

I Bonds are a low-risk, liquid savings choice. The interest rate has both fixed and variable rate components. The variable rate is adjusted periodically based on the current inflation rate. The minimum purchase is $25 (for a $25 bond) online. I Bonds are often used to pay for college education. If used for this purpose, they may not be subject to federal taxes. Minimum ownership is one year, but they earn interest for 30 years. There are penalties for selling these bonds before 5 years.

EE Bonds carry a fixed rate of interest. They are safe, low-risk savings bonds. Their guaranteed rate of interest is competitive with market rates. To finance education, EE Bonds are a great option. EE Bonds are discount bonds. You can buy a $50 EE Bond for $25. When maturity is reached, the bond continues earning interest for a total of 30 years. You can buy, manage, and sell EE Bonds directly from your home computer. EE Bonds can be purchased for education purposes. If so, earnings may not be taxable.

All of these securities are loans to the U.S. government. You can buy them directly from the TreasuryDirect website or from a bank. Some items are discounted (sold at less than face value), and some are not. All of them are long-term savings options that are safe. Treasury securities can be sold at any time, but there are interest penalties if you sell them before maturity.

Questions

1. Where do you buy U.S. Treasury securities? How do you do it?

2. How are Treasury bills different from Treasury notes?

3. What is meant by buying at a discount?

4. How are I Bonds different from EE Bonds?

5. U.S. Treasury savings choices are subject to some income taxes but not others. Explain.

6. Would you consider buying a U.S. Treasury security? Why or why not?

EXERCISE 5-5   Building Math Skills: Growing Savings

Directions: Compute the following problems using the simple interest formula, the compound interest method, and the Rule of 72, as shown in Chapter 5 of your textbook.

1.   Selena has placed $500 in an account that pays simple interest of 5 percent annually. How much interest will Selena have earned by the end of the year?

2.   Suki has placed $800 in an account that pays 4 percent interest compounded quarterly. What will be the balance in the account at the end of 2 years (8 quarters)? How much interest will Suki have earned during that time? Round your answers to the nearest cent. (Round up if a number is 5 or higher.)

Year	Beginning Balance	Rate 4%	Qtr. 1	Qtr. 2	Qtr. 3	Qtr. 4	Ending Balance
1							
2							

3.   Jessica is considering putting $50 into a money market account that pays a 4 percent annual interest rate. How long will it take for the money to double to $100? Use the Rule of 72 to find the answer.

EXERCISE 5-6   Building Math Skills: Compound Interest

Directions: Complete the following tables showing different savings options. Round your answers to the nearest cent. (Round up if a number is 5 or higher.) You can do the math manually or use a spreadsheet program.

1. You plan to set aside $500 for 5 years. The account pays annual interest of 8 percent, compounded quarterly. What is the ending balance (principal plus interest) at the end of 5 years?

Year	Beginning Balance	Rate 8%	Qtr. 1	Qtr. 2	Qtr. 3	Qtr. 4	Ending Balance
1							
2							
3							
4							
5							

2. You have savings of $100. You plan to save another $100 at the beginning of each year for 5 years. The account pays annual interest of 8 percent, compounded quarterly. What is the ending balance (principal plus interest) at the end of 5 years?

Year	Beginning Balance	Yearly Payment	Rate 8%	Qtr. 1	Qtr. 2	Qtr. 3	Qtr. 4	Ending Balance
1								
2								
3								
4								
5								

EXERCISE 5-7   Building Math Skills: Future Value

Directions: Answer the following questions using the future value tables shown in your textbook in Figure 5-2.3, Future Value (Compound Sum) of $1, and Figure 5.2-4, Future Value of an Annuity. The Future Value (Compound Sum) of $1 table is used when saving a single sum. The Future Value of an Annuity table is used when saving a fixed amount on a regular basis.

1.   How much money will you have in six years if you set aside $5,000 at 8%?

2.   How much money will you have in 10 years if you set aside $1,000 at 10%?

3.   How much money will you have in 20 years if you set aside $2,000 at 8%?

4.   How much money will you have in five years if you set aside $1,000 a year at 8%?

5.   How much money will you have in ten years if you set aside $500 a year at 10%?

6.   How much money will you have in 15 years if you set aside $100 a year at 6%?

7.   How much money will you have in 20 years if you set aside $1,000 a year at 8%?

EXERCISE 5-8   Careers in Banking

Directions: The banking or financial services industry has many career positions available. Some of them are described below. Read the job duties for each position. Then answer the questions that follow.

Customer service representative (also known as bank teller)	Assists customers with deposits, withdrawals, opening and closing accounts, and other transactions such as purchasing cashier's checks or accessing a safe deposit box
Bank branch manager	Supervises customer service representatives; provides transaction approvals; represents the branch to the public; is responsible for reaching branch profit goals
Personal loan officer	Works with customers to process loan applications and obtain approval from underwriters/loan committees; analyzes application data and approves/rejects loan applications
Mortgage underwriter	Matches loan applicants with mortgage lenders based on selection criteria; is responsible for selecting qualified borrowers who will meet loan obligations
Vice president, banking operations	Supervises branch managers and profits for a group of banks; is responsible for profits in a geographic area
Commercial loan officer	Works with businesses to process applications for business loans and obtain approval from underwriters/loan committees; analyzes application data and approves/rejects loan applications
Internal auditor	Responsible for checking and verifying accuracy of records and procedures; makes sure processes are being followed and financial reports reflect true results of operations

1. Which of these positions sounds the most interesting to you? Why?

2. What aspects of this type of work do you find most appealing? Why?

3. Access the *Occupational Outlook Handbook* online. Search for banking careers. Find at least two job titles that are the same as or similar to those listed above. What is the expected salary for each position?

EXERCISE 5-9   Checkbook Register

Directions: Make the following entries into the checkbook register on the next page. Keep a running balance.

1. Beginning checkbook balance: $124.18

2. January 14   Check No. 143   Del's Market   For groceries $48.12

3. January 16   Check No. 144   Chuck Smith   For loan payment $50.00

4. January 18   Debit purchase   Burger Queen   For food $8.95

5. January 19   Deposit   Payroll check $116.82

6. January 23   Check No. 145   Far West Power Co.   For utilities $35.00

7. January 25   Check No. 146   Westmore High School   For fees $14.00

8. January 28   ATM withdrawal   For spending money $40.00

9. January 30   Debit purchase   DelMart   For supplies $17.85

10. February 2   Deposit   Payroll check $115.90

11. February 6   Online payment   CableVision   For movies rented $22.00

12. February 9   Check No. 147   Harrisville Bakery   For order $19.00

13. February 9   Service fee $9.00

DC-Debit Card Purchase		DEP-Deposit	ON-Online Payment		WD-ATM Withdrawal		SC-Service Charge	
CHECK NO. OR CODE	DATE	DESCRIPTION OF TRANSACTION	PAYMENT/ DEBIT (−)	FEE (−)	√	DEPOSIT/ CREDIT (+)	BALANCE	

EXERCISE 5-10   Bank Reconciliation

Directions: A checkbook register for your account is shown below and a bank statement is shown on the next page. Complete the bank reconciliation using the form provided on page 77. The bank reconciliation date is July 3. Remember to update the checkbook register.

Checkbook Register

DC-Debit Card Purchase	DEP-Deposit		ON-Online Payment		WD-ATM Withdrawal		SC-Service Charge

CHECK NO. OR CODE	DATE	DESCRIPTION OF TRANSACTION	PAYMENT/ DEBIT (–)	FEE (–)	√	DEPOSIT/ CREDIT (+)	BALANCE
							136.54
144	6/12	Fredrick's Market	22.16				22.16
		Food					114.38
145	6/14	Gray's Maintenance	35.00				35.00
		Repairs					79.38
DC	6/15	Gaming Arcade	15.00				15.00
		Entertainment					64.38
WD	6/18	Withdrawal of Cash	25.00				25.00
		ATM (no fee)					39.38
DEP	6/22	Deposit				111.28	111.28
		Paycheck					150.66
146	6/26	Dad	50.00				50.00
		Loan Payment					100.66
147	6/30	Fredrick's Market	11.85				11.85
		Food					88.81
148	7/1	DayMart	24.12				24.12
		Supplies					64.69

BANK STATEMENT

Farmer's Bank
Middlefield, Ohio

Student Name
125 Fourth Street
Middlefield, OH 44062-1250

Account No.   78953-4

Statement Date   06/30/20—

Balance from Previous Statement	Amount of Deposits and Credits	Amount of Withdrawals and Debits	Amount of Charges	Statement Balance
136.54	111.28	147.16	8.00	92.66

Date	Code	Transaction Description	Transaction Amount
Checks			
6/12/20--	144	Fredrick's Market	22.16
6/14/20--	145	Gray's Maintenance	35.00
6/26/20--	146	Albert Jones	50.00
Other Debits			
6/15/20--	DC	Gaming Arcade	15.00
6/18/20--	ATM	ATM Withdrawal	25.00
Deposits			
6/22/20	DEP	Deposit	111.28
Fees			
6/30/20--	SC	Checking Account Fee	8.00

RECONCILIATION OF BANK STATEMENT

Date _____   Account No. _____

Bank Statement Balance on   _____ $_____

Add Deposits in Transit and Other Credits

Date	Amount

                        Total Deposits in Transit/Credits   _____

                        Subtotal $_____

Deduct Outstanding Checks/Withdrawals

Check No.	Date	Amount

                Total Outstanding Checks/Withdrawals   _____

Adjusted Bank Balance $_____

Checkbook Register Balance on   _____ $_____

Deduct Bank Charges

Description	Amount

                        Total Bank Charges   _____

                        Subtotal $_____

Add Interest or Other Credits

Description	Amount

                        Total Credits   _____

Adjusted Checkbook Register Balance $_____

CHAPTER 6
Personal Risk Management

EXERCISE 6-1 Review of Chapter Key Terms

Directions: Write the letter of the correct definition beside its corresponding term.

_____ 1. automobile insurance

_____ 2. beneficiary

_____ 3. disability insurance

_____ 4. health insurance

_____ 5. home inventory

_____ 6. homeowner's insurance

_____ 7. liability coverage

_____ 8. life insurance

_____ 9. loss

_____ 10. permanent life insurance

_____ 11. premium

_____ 12. probability

_____ 13. renter's insurance

_____ 14. risk

_____ 15. risk assessment

_____ 16. risk reduction

_____ 17. risk transfer

_____ 18. self-insure

_____ 19. stop-loss provision

_____ 20. term life insurance

_____ 21. umbrella policy

A. Insurance that provides income to replace a portion of normal earnings when the insured is unable to work due to nonwork-related injury or illness

B. A physical injury, damage to property, or disappearance of property

C. Insurance that protects a car owner from losses as a result of accidents and other events

D. The process of identifying risks and deciding how serious they are

E. Liability coverage above that of homeowner's and car insurance

F. The price paid for insurance coverage

G. A clause that provides 100 percent coverage of medical expenses after a certain amount has been paid

H. Insurance that provides a death benefit and builds cash value

I. A tenant's policy that protects against the loss of personal property in a rented residence

J. A list of items of value in your home

K. Buying insurance to shift the risk of financial loss

L. Temporary insurance that pays only a death benefit

M. The person designated to receive money from a life insurance policy

N. Insurance that protects against risk of loss to a home and its contents

O. The chance of injury, damage, or economic loss

P. Insurance that pays money to the beneficiary upon the death of the insured person

Q. Setting aside money to be used in the event of injury or loss

R. A plan for sharing the risk of medical costs

S. Finding ways to lower your chance of incurring a loss

T. Insurance protection against injuries suffered by others on your property or as a result of your actions

U. The liklihood of a risk resulting in a loss

Directions: Write the letter "T" for a true statement or "F" for a false statement.

_____ 22. All risks have serious potential losses and should be managed with risk avoidance or risk transfer.

_____ 23. Driving without a spare tire will usually lead to serious personal risk.

_____ 24. Having a home security alarm system can reduce your insurance premium.

_____ 25. You should assume the risk for large expenses and get insurance to cover small and routine costs.

_____ 26. If you have health insurance, you do not have to worry about the costs of health care.

_____ 27. A major advantage to HMOs is their focus on preventive care and wellness.

_____ 28. Term insurance is an important part of your permanent life insurance plan.

_____ 29. Homeowner's insurance protects a homeowner from fire damage but does not include liability coverage.

_____ 30. High-risk pools offer maximum insurance coverage at high cost to poor drivers.

_____ 31. You can reduce your insurance premium cost by paying annually instead of monthly.

EXERCISE 6-3 Multiple Choice Questions

Directions: Write the letter of the correct answer in the space provided.

_____ 32. Finding ways to lower your chance of loss is (a) risk avoidance, (b) risk reduction, (c) risk transfer, (d) risk assumption

_____ 33. Not participating in a dangerous activity is (a) risk avoidance, (b) risk reduction, (c) risk transfer, (d) risk assumption

_____ 34. Self-insuring is a form of (a) risk avoidance, (b) risk reduction, (c) risk transfer, (d) risk assumption

_____ 35. Which of the following is considered unmanaged care? (a) PPO, (b) HMO, (c) fee-for-service, (d) all of the above

_____ 36. Which of the following type of health insurance plan includes coverage for medical, hospital, and surgery expenses? (a) major medical, (b) basic health care, (c) catastrophic illness, (d) short-term disability

_____ 37. Temporary coverage for nonwork-related illness or injury is covered by (a) basic health care, (b) short-term disability insurance, (c) long-term disability insurance, (d) major medical

_____ 38. Which of the following is known as pure insurance? (a) whole life insurance, (b) term insurance, (c) permanent insurance, (d) universal life insurance

_____ 39. In which type of term insurance policy will the death benefit remain the same? (a) renewable term, (b) decreasing term, (c) level term, (d) all of the above

_____ 40. Which of the following type of coverage would pay for injuries to guests in your home? (a) liability coverage, (b) vandalism coverage, (c) fire insurance, (d) acts of nature coverage

_____ 41. For insurance purposes, what you would pay today to replace an item is the (a) actual cash value, (b) replacement cost, (c) limited cost, (d) real property value

EXERCISE 6-4   Building Communications Skills: Reading

To remember important information (for high-concentration reading), you can use patterns. One pattern is called an acrostic. With an acrostic, letters spell a special word. The word you create reminds you of the main points to remember. For example, some key ways to lower insurance costs could be summarized in the acrostic CLASP, as follows:

C	**Compare**	Comparison shop for insurance. There are many insurance companies to choose from. Find those that offer the best rates.
L	**Look**	Look for discount opportunities. Nonsmokers may get lower premiums on health and life insurance. Taking a driver training program and getting good grades can reduce car insurance costs. Some groups such as credit unions offer discount insurance rates.
A	**Accept**	Accept higher deductibles. The higher the deductible, the lower the premium. You can save money using this self-insuring technique in areas where you can reduce or avoid risks.
S	**Seek**	Seek group insurance. Group plans are usually much lower than individual plans. Look for groups—at work, credit unions, social organizations, and other places. You'll save money on premiums.
P	**Payments**	Monthly payments usually have an extra fee. If you pay premiums twice a year, you can reduce your costs. You can also save by having payments deducted automatically from your checking account.

Directions: Read a passage with material you want to remember. Form an acrostic, and write its main points here.

EXERCISE 6-5   Building Math Skills: Coinsurance

Some homeowner's policies have a coinsurance clause. This clause requires that you buy coverage equal to a stated percentage of the property's value. If you do not have at least that amount of coverage, you will not get full payment should a loss occur.

For example, an 80 percent coinsurance clause would require the following insurance for a house worth $200,000:

$200,000 × 0.8 = $160,000 coverage required

Many homeowners believe they can save money by underinsuring. The owners of this $200,000 house may decide they can save money by buying insurance for only $120,000 rather than the required $160,000. The owners reason that if they have a fire that causes anything less than $120,000 in damage, they will get full payment. However, that is not how the coverage works.

Assume they have a fire, and the damage is $60,000. The house is insured for $120,000, which is 75 percent of the required coverage ($120,000 ÷ $160,000). Thus, the insurance company would pay $45,000, which is 75 percent of the loss ($60,000 × 0.75).

Directions: Complete the following problems using the examples discussed above.

1. A house worth $250,000 has a coinsurance clause of 90 percent. The owners insure the property for $191,250. They then have a fire that causes $80,000 in damage. How much money will they receive from insurance?

2. A house worth $180,000 has a coinsurance clause of 75 percent. The owners insure the property for $101,250. They then have a loss that results in a $50,000 claim. How much money will they receive from insurance?

EXERCISE 6-6   Careers in Risk Management

Directions: Several career positions are available in risk management such as those listed below. Choose one of these jobs or another job related to risk management and conduct research. You can find information about careers in the *Occupational Outlook Handbook*. Then answer the questions that follow.

- Investment adviser
- Insurance agent/broker
- Personal banker
- Securities account manager

1.   What are the main duties or functions of this job?

2.   What type of education or training is required for this job?

3.   What is the average salary for this job?

4.   What is the job outlook for this career?

5.   Would a career in this field interest you? Why or why not?

EXERCISE 6-7   Risk Assessment

Directions: The following table lists five types of risks a typical person might face. Identify the seriousness of each risk by rating it from 1 to 10, with 1 being a low risk and 10 being a high risk. For each risk, list strategies a person could use to reduce, avoid, or transfer the risk.

RISK	SERIOUSNESS RATING	WAYS TO REDUCE, AVOID, OR TRANSFER RISK
1. Boating injuries		
2. Bicycle injuries		
3. Loss of personal property due to theft from a car		
4. Loss of income due to short-term disability resulting from an injury at home		
5. Loss resulting from a car accident		

EXERCISE 6-8   Teen Drivers

Teen drivers have the highest crash risk of any age group. Per mile traveled, they also have the highest accident involvement rate. These accidents range from simple "fender benders" to fatal crashes. You can find information about teen drivers on the Internet. Practical information about driving safely is also available.

Directions: Access the Internet and find answers to the following questions. One website that you may find helpful is the Insurance Institute for Highway Safety site. Other sites also offer useful information. Search the Web using terms such as *teen drivers* and *driving safety* to find other sites.

1.   Find vehicle ratings, and briefly summarize rating information for one vehicle.

2.   Find statistics about teen drivers. Write down two interesting statistics that you find.

3.   Look for information such as consumer brochures and videos. List types of information you find that are available to consumers and teachers.

EXERCISE 6-9   Ethics

Directions: When people drive, they must be responsible for their actions. Many driving-related activities involve ethical issues. Read about the ethical issues described below and then answer the questions that follow. If needed, use the Internet to conduct additional research on the topics.

Driving Accidents

Most states have financial responsibility laws. These laws may require that drivers be insured or that they be able to pay for damages caused to others. The minimum coverage required in many states is liability insurance. Liability insurance protects others from the results of negligence. In spite of legal requirements, many people drive without insurance. Some cite the high cost of insurance as their reason. Because of uninsured motorists, drivers often buy extra insurance coverage to protect against losses from an accident with one of them. Driving without insurance or without the means to pay for damages you cause to others is unethical.

1.   Explain how financial responsibility laws protect all drivers and how you would deal with drivers who refuse to obey this law.

Faking Injuries

When you injure another person in an accident, you can be sued for damages. Sometimes people demand money even though they have not been injured. They fake injuries in order to get money from the insurance company. This practice is both illegal and unethical.

2.   Explain why it is unethical to fake injuries. Who gets hurt?

Staging Accidents

There are people who stage accidents, causing your vehicle to rear-end theirs. When you hit another car from the rear, you are presumed guilty in many states. Always drive very carefully. Leave lots of room between you and the car in front of you. Defensive driving is a driving skill that helps you be aware of other vehicles and to react positively in certain traffic situations. Taking a defensive driving course can help to lessen the risk of loss from automobile accidents.

3. Explain how another person can stage an accident. When you are presumed to be at fault, what can you do to protect yourself? Research defensive driving techniques online and list some tips.

Underinsuring

One of the most common problems today is getting into an accident in which the driver at fault does not have enough insurance coverage to pay for the damages that she or he caused. You can protect yourself with uninsured/underinsured motorist coverage.

4. Explain why it is unethical to have too little insurance (underinsuring). Research and list the costs of adding uninsured/underinsured motorist coverage to an auto insurance policy.

EXERCISE 6-10 Insurance Needs and Costs

Directions: Read each of the scenarios below and determine the best way to meet insurance needs.

1. You are considering whether to buy a whole life or a term life insurance policy. The death benefit will be the same for each policy. The premiums for the whole life policy will be $600 a year. In 40 years you will be able to withdraw the cash value of $50,000 from the policy. The premiums for a 40-year term policy will be $200 a year. You would invest the money you save on premiums and receive an average annual return of at least 6 percent on the money you save for the next 40 years. Which option would you choose? Why? (Hint: Search for a Future Value of an Annuity of $1 table online to compute the earnings from your savings.)

2. Ramon Caldez is 30 years old. He is married and has one son, who is 3 years old. Ramon earns $40,000 a year in gross pay. Ramon's wife stays at home to care for their son and earns no income. He and his wife own their home, which is valued at $100,000. Ramon thinks the contents of their home would be valued at about $50,000. They have two cars. One car is new and has a 4-year loan. The other car is 10 years old and needs to be replaced.

    a. What type of health insurance coverage would you advise Ramon to get for himself and his family?

    b. Ramon has short-term disability insurance provided by his employer. He wants to add long-term disability coverage. What amount of monthly benefit would you advise Ramon to have in the long-term disability policy?

c. Ramon's employer provides life insurance for him equal to 25 percent of his annual gross salary. How much life insurance coverage does Ramon have through his employer? Should Ramon buy additional life insurance to protect his family? Would you advise that he buy term life insurance or whole life insurance? Why?

d. What does Ramon need to do before deciding how much homeowner's insurance he needs? Ramon's home is in an area with a high danger of flooding. Is flood protection likely to be covered in his homeowner's policy? If not, how can he get flood protection?

e. Ramon has a car loan for his new car. Ramon owns the car that is 10 years old. What type of auto insurance would you recommend Ramon carry on each car?

CHAPTER 7
Buying Decisions

EXERCISE 7-1   Review of Chapter Key Terms

Directions: Write the letter of the correct definition beside its corresponding term.

_____ 1.   access checks

_____ 2.   balance transfer

_____ 3.   buying plan

_____ 4.   cancellation fee

_____ 5.   charge card

_____ 6.   collateral

_____ 7.   consumer loan

_____ 8.   credit

_____ 9.   criteria

_____ 10. extended warranty

_____ 11. financial responsibility

_____ 12. fixed interest rate

_____ 13. installment credit

_____ 14. introductory rate

_____ 15. line of credit

_____ 16. minimum payment

_____ 17. over-the-limit fee

_____ 18. penalty

_____ 19. rebate

_____ 20. revolving credit

_____ 21. service credit

_____ 22. spending limit

_____ 23. store account

_____ 24. variable interest rate

A. A preapproved loan amount that can be borrowed against

B. The ability to receive services and pay for them later

C. Interest rate that can change at any time without notice

D. The ability to borrow money and pay it back later

E. A fee charged for violating a credit agreement

F. Being able to meet your financial goals through planned earning, spending, and saving

G. Temporary, low-interest rate offered when you open a new account

H. An account on which the account holder can charge repeatedly up to a maximum limit

I. Checks provided by a credit card company that allow you to borrow against your credit card account

J. Credit account that allows you to charge items or services only at a specific store or merchant

K. Interest rate that does not change from month to month

L. A penalty charged for exceeding the approved credit limit

M. Standards or rules by which something is judged

N. Credit used to finance a single high-priced item through a series of equal payments made over a set period of time

O. A direct loan of cash made to a consumer at a fixed interest rate for a set period of time

P. The maximum amount you are willing to pay for an item

Q. Property used as security for a loan

R. A refund of part of the purchase price of an item

S. Additional coverage that you can buy to pay for repairs or replacements needed beyond the original warranty period

T. Moving a balance from one credit card account to another

U. Form of credit card where the balance is paid in full each month

V. The amount you are required to pay each month on a credit account

W. A penalty for closing your account prior to a stated period

X. Organized method for making good buying decisions

Directions: Write the letter "T" for a true statement or "F" for a false statement.

_____ **25.** Being financially responsible means you are able to make payments as agreed and honor your financial commitments.

_____ **26.** Financial irresponsibility leads to more fun, less risk, and lack of stress in your life.

_____ **27.** When defining your spending goal, you should recognize your opportunity cost.

_____ **28.** The lowest price for a good or service is always the best price.

_____ **29.** When making a purchase, the return policy is not an important consideration.

_____ **30.** The person who borrows money or uses credit is a debtor.

_____ **31.** Credit cards usually require that you make a minimum monthly payment.

_____ **32.** VISA and Mastercard are examples of charge cards.

_____ **33.** Loans with collateral have lower interest rates because of lower risk to the lender.

_____ **34.** Small businesses often rely heavily on their line of credit.

_____ **35.** With a rewards feature, you can get money back for using your credit card.

_____ **36.** Your FICO score is not important when you are being considered for a new loan or credit card.

_____ **37.** Creditors can never raise the interest rate on a credit card account with a fixed rate.

_____ **38.** Payday loans are a form of easy access credit.

EXERCISE 7-3   Multiple Choice Questions

Directions: Write the letter of the correct answer in the space provided.

_____ **39.** What is the first step of a buying plan? (a) define a spending goal, (b) list items that will meet the goal, (c) describe features of the ideal choice, (d) set a timeline

_____ **40.** A buying plan should always include (a) spending limits, (b) criteria, (c) comparison shopping, (d) all of the above

_____ **41.** A lender is also called a(n) (a) creditor, (b) debtor, (c) borrower, (d) consumer

_____ **42.** Visiting a doctor and paying later involves which type of credit? (a) revolving, (b) installment, (c) service, (d) charge card

_____ **43.** VISA and MasterCard are examples of (a) store cards, (b) credit cards, (c) charge cards, (d) installment credit

_____ **44.** A person who signs a loan agreement with the borrower and agrees to repay the loan if the borrower does not is a(n) (a) creditor, (b) cosigner, (c) lender, (d) collateral

_____ **45.** Which of the following is *not* a major credit bureau? (a) TransUnion, (b) Experian, (c) Equifax, (d) Fair Isaac and Company

_____ **46.** Information related to a bankruptcy stays in your credit file for how long? (a) 90 days, (b) 180 days, (c) 3 years, (d) 10 years

_____ **47.** What carries the most weight when calculating A FICO score? (a) payment history, (b) amounts owed, (c) length of credit history, (d) new credit issued

_____ **48.** Interest and fees are also known as (a) debt, (b) finance charges, (c) variable rates, (d) fixed rates

EXERCISE 7-4   Building Communications Skills: Informal Speaking

Directions: Work in a group with five classmates. Each person will speak informally about one of the topics listed below. Choose who will discuss each topic. The purpose of the speech is to inform. Sitting in a circle, express your ideas clearly, get feedback, and finish your speech based on feedback (verbal and nonverbal) from the other students. Each person has 5 minutes to present his or her topic.

Person #1:   The topic is a camping trip you plan to take.

Person #2:   The topic is a class activity you plan to work on.

Person #3:   The topic is a seminar you would like to take or a special skill you would like to develop.

Person #4:   The topic is a book you read recently.

Person #5:   The topic is a current event you read about in the newspaper or heard about on the radio or TV.

EXERCISE 7-5   Building Math Skills: Calculating Interest

Directions: Examine the credit card information shown below. Compute the interest charge and the new balance (amount owed) using the three different methods of computing interest. Use spreadsheet software, if it is available.

Previous Balance	$500	

Purchases
    May 12
    May 22
    May 30
	
	$25
	$100
	$50	

Payment May 20	$110	
Interest Rate	12% per year (1% per month)	

1. Adjusted Balance Method

    Interest _____

    New Balance _____

2. Previous Balance Method

    Interest _____

    New Balance _____

3. Average Daily Balance Method

    Interest _____

    New Balance _____

EXERCISE 7-6   Buying Plan

Directions: Using the chart below, define three spending goals (needs or wants you are trying to meet). Then identify three items you plan to purchase, either soon or sometime in the future, to satisfy your goals. List buying criteria (features you want to have) for each item. Set a timeline and a spending limit for each item.

SPENDING GOAL	ITEM	CRITERIA	TIMELINE	SPENDING LIMIT
1.				
2.				
3.				

EXERCISE 7-7   Use of Credit

Directions: For each of the numbered situations listed below, assume some form of credit is used. Identify which of the following options would be most appropriate for the situation:

- Charge card

- Revolving credit (credit card)

- Installment credit

- Service credit

- Line of credit

Note: More than one option may be appropriate for a single purchase. List all that would be appropriate.

1. Purchase of a new bicycle   _____

2. Purchase of a house   _____

3. Purchase of groceries   _____

4. Receipt of utility bill   _____

5. Purchase of a car   _____

6. Purchase of a birthday gift   _____

7. Dinner at a restaurant   _____

8. Purchase of clothing   _____

9. Purchase of gasoline   _____

10. Dental appointment   _____

EXERCISE 7-8   Credit Application

Directions: To get a credit card or open a store account, consumers typically must fill out a credit application. Although you may not be ready to apply for credit for a few years, practice completing the credit application on the next page using the following information. Print the data neatly and clearly on the form.

1. Enter your title (Mr., Mrs., Ms., Miss), name, and address.
2. For a home phone, enter **606-555-4321**; for a business phone, enter **606-555-0132**.
3. For the date of birth, enter **August 1, 1985**.
4. Enter **0** for the number of dependents.
5. For a social security number, enter **000-111-0000**.
6. For an e-mail address, enter **myname@provider.com**.
7. Indicate that you are a U.S. citizen.
8. Indicate that you rent your residence and pay **$600** per month in rent.
9. For your employer, enter the name of a business in your area. Use the real address of the business or make up an address.
10. In the *Occupation* box, enter a job that would be held by someone at this business. Indicate that you have worked there for **4** years.
11. For the name of a supervisor, enter **Emily Gale**.
12. You earn $10 per hour, working 40 hours per week for 50 weeks a year. Compute your gross pay, and enter it in the *Yearly Gross Pay* box. Enter the same amount in the *Yearly Household Income* box.
13. Enter **None** in the *Other Income* box.
14. In the first *Other Credit Accounts* box, enter **Sears** in the *Type or Name* box. Enter **34289-10** for the account number. Enter **$250** for the current balance.
15. Under *Bank Accounts*, place a check mark to indicate that you have a checking account. Write the name of a local bank. Write the name of your city or a nearby city. For the account number, write **45892-4509**.
16. Indicate that you have a savings account at the same local bank. For the account number, write **45892-4510**.
17. Sign your name and enter the current date at the bottom of the form.

CREDIT APPLICATION

PARNELL BANK

PERSONAL DATA

___ Mr. ___ Ms. ___ Mrs. ___ Miss	First Name		Middle	Last Name

Home Address	City		State	ZIP Code	How long?

Previous Address (If less than 2 years at present address)		City	State	ZIP Code

Home Telephone	Business Telephone	Date of Birth	No. of Dependents

Social Security No.	E-Mail Address

Are you a U.S. citizen? ___ Yes ___ No	If no, explain status.	Residence Situation ___ Own ___ Rent ___ Other	Monthly Rent or Mortgage $

Employment

Employer	Address	City	State	ZIP Code

How long?	Occupation	Supervisor's Name	Yearly Gross Pay $

Other Income Amount Source	Amount Source	Yearly Household Income $

Other Credit Accounts

Type or Name	Account No.	Current Balance $
Type or Name	Account No.	Current Balance $
Type or Name	Account No.	Current Balance $

Bank Accounts

___ Checking Name of Bank	City	Account No.
___ Savings Name of Bank	City	Account No.
___ Other Name of Bank	City	Account No.

Signature

I authorize Parnell Bank to check my credit record and verify my employment and references. I have read the information on the reverse side and agree to the credit terms. Under penalties of perjury, I declare the above statements to be true.

_____   Date _____
Applicant's Signature

EXERCISE 7-9   Credit Report

Directions: Based on the partial credit report below, answer the questions that follow.

PERSONAL CREDIT REPORT

Prepared for:	Report Date:	Report Number:	Summary of Information:		FICO:
Bill Smythe	3/15/2011	32461	Public records:	2	585
			Accounts:	4	
			Accounts in good standing:	3	

Public Record Information:

Source	Date Filed	Account	Amount	Comments
1. County Cthse	3/2010	Joint	$4,000	Lawsuit filed District Court
2. US Dist Ct	6/2008	Joint	$33,000	Repossession/ vehicle 6/2009

Credit Information:

Source of Credit	Date Opened/ Last Report		Account Type	Type/ Payment	High/Current Balance	Current Status
3. Miami Bank	6/03	2/11	Individual	Loan $100 min	$2,000/$1,800	Late 2 pmts
4. C&C Credit	4/10	1/11	Joint	Install. $250/mo	$5,500/$5,100	Current
5. Bls Mortgage	3/08	2/11	Joint	Mortgage $822/mo	$118,000/$111,000	Current
6. BVD Cable	2/10	2/11	Individual	Open $107/mo	$214/$0	Current

1.   For whom is this report prepared?

2.   What is this person's FICO score? Is this a good score? Explain.

3.   Why do you think the FICO score is at this level?

4.   How could this person's credit score be improved?

CHAPTER 8
Preserving Your Credit

EXERCISE 8-1   Review of Chapter Key Terms

Directions: Write the letter of the correct definition beside its corresponding term.

_____	1.	advance-fee loan
_____	2.	annual fee
_____	3.	balloon payment
_____	4.	billing cycle
_____	5.	consideration
_____	6.	consumer finance company
_____	7.	contract
_____	8.	debt repayment plan
_____	9.	down payment
_____	10.	eviction
_____	11.	grace period
_____	12.	lease
_____	13.	living habits
_____	14.	loan shark
_____	15.	logistics
_____	16.	market value
_____	17.	mortgage
_____	18.	prepayment penalty
_____	19.	property manager
_____	20.	refinancing
_____	21.	roommate
_____	22.	sales finance company
_____	23.	security deposit
_____	24.	trade-in
_____	25.	unused credit

A. A person who offers illegal, unsecured loans

B. The amount of time you have to pay your credit card bill without having to pay interest on new purchases

C. Your daily routine

D. A loan that includes a large upfront fee

E. A large lump-sum payment that must be paid at a set time

F. Difference between your credit limit and current balance

G. Strategy for paying off debt and reducing total interest paid

H. A rental agreement that specifies the rights and duties of the landlord and tenant

I. Time period during which you must make your payment

J. The act of making a plan and carrying it out

K. A long-term debt agreement used to purchase real estate

L. A lender that extends high-interest loans to consumers who may be ineligible for other types of loans

M. A legally binding agreement

N. A person hired to take care of rental property and communicate with tenants

O. A lender that makes loans for the purchase of consumer goods, often working closely with the seller

P. Something of value applied toward the down payment of a new purchase

Q. A fee charged if you repay a loan before the agreed-upon time

R. A yearly charge to your credit card account for membership

S. The process of expelling a tenant from rented property

T. The highest price a property will bring on the open market

U. A cash deposit paid toward the purchase price

V. A person with whom you share living space

W. A refundable amount paid to cover damages to property caused by a tenant

X. Paying off an old loan by taking out a new loan

Y. Something of value exchanged for something else of value

Directions: Write the letter "T" for a true statement or "F" for a false statement.

_____ 26.   A landlord is a person who pays rent under the terms of a lease agreement.

_____ 27.   Moving costs include packing, loading, transporting, unloading and unpacking, as well as installation and other fees and deposits.

_____ 28.   Tenants can be evicted if they fail to live up to their contractual duties.

_____ 29.   Typically car loans and other installment loans do not require a down payment from the buyer.

_____ 30.   When you lease a car, you will not be responsible for major repair costs.

_____ 31.   Owning your own house gives you tax advantages, such as deductible property taxes and interest expense.

_____ 32.   All student loans involve deferred payments and accrued interest.

_____ 33.   Increasing your monthly payment will help you pay off your debt quicker but will not reduce the total interest you pay.

_____ 34.   A rent-to-own agreement for personal property is usually a much more expensive option than traditional methods of buying.

_____ 35.   Your debt load is the amount of outstanding debt at a particular time.

EXERCISE 8-3   **Multiple Choice Questions**

Directions: Write the letter of the correct answer in the space provided.

_____ 36.   Interest rates are rising during (a) economic growth, (b) economic slowdown, (c) both a and b, (d) neither a or b

_____ 37.   Which of the following credit card features will *not* reduce your cost of credit? (a) cash rebates, (b) rewards, (c) annual fee, (d) low interest rate

_____ 38.   Which of the following is *not* a type of living habit? (a) cleanliness, (b) sleeping late, (c) frequent socializing, (d) vehicle used for transportation

_____ 39.   Which of the following is refundable to the tenant? (a) cleaning fee, (b) monthly rent, (c) service fee, (d) security deposit

_____ 40.   Landlords are responsible for all of the following *except* (a) monitoring guests, (b) fixing plumbing problems, (c) repairing roofs, (d) providing door locks

_____ 41.   The process of dividing up your debt into equal payments is (a) depreciation, (b) preapproval, (c) amortization, (d) refinancing

_____ 42.   Which of the following is an advantage of home ownership? (a) property taxes deduction, (b) appreciation, (c) equity, (d) all of the above

_____ 43.   Which of the following would *not* require a down payment? (a) car loan, (b) house loan, (c) business startup loan, (d) student loan

_____ 44.   If you had a loan for $30,000 at an annual interest rate of 8% with a 90-day interest prepayment penalty, what would be the amount of your penalty? (a) $200, (b) $400, (c) $600, (d) $2,400

_____ 45.   Laws that set the maximum rate of interest that can be charged are called (a) credit billing laws, (b) usury laws, (c) consumer protection laws, (d) there are no such laws

EXERCISE 8-4   Building Communications Skills: Formal Speaking

Directions: Giving a speech in front of an audience can be a very rewarding experience. Learning to speak effectively is an important skill that will be valuable at school and at work. Prepare a 5-minute speech and present it to a class or small group of people. Follow these steps:

1. Choose a topic that can be presented in 5 minutes. The purpose of the speech can be to inform, to entertain, or to persuade. Ask your teacher to approve the topic.

2. Create an outline of the speech. Include an introduction, a body, and a conclusion. Then write detailed notes about what you will say. Consider the audience and what these listeners will know about the topic as you write the speech. Prepare electronic slides, transparencies, posters, handouts, or other aids that you can use during the speech delivery.

3. Time the speech so that you can present it in not less than 4 minutes and 50 seconds or more than 5 minutes and 10 seconds.

4. Practice the speech in front of a group of people.

    •   Dress appropriately.

    •   Maintain eye contact. Use visual aids, if appropriate.

    •   Speak slowly and steadily; keep your voice firm.

    •   Be relaxed and comfortable; smile and use humor if appropriate.

5. Critique your own presentation, and receive feedback from the audience.

    •   What did you do well?

    •   What could be improved?

    •   What would you do differently next time?

6. Submit the speech outline and your critique of your delivery of the speech to your teacher.

EXERCISE 8-5   Building Math Skills: Annual Percentage Rates

The annual percentage rate (APR) of a loan takes into account the other loan fees, such as closing costs and loan application fees, that a borrower must pay in addition to paying interest on the principal borrowed. Comparing the APRs for two different loans can help you determine which loan has the highest total costs. When comparing the APRs for loan offers, be sure the same fees are covered in the APR numbers. APR calculators, available on the Internet, can be used to find the APR for a loan. To find an APR calculator, you can enter the term *APR calculator* into a search engine.

You can also calculate the approximate APR manually. For example, suppose you buy a sofa with a cash price of $800.00. You make a down payment of $100.00 and take out an installment loan of $700.00 to cover the remainder. You will make 12 payments of $66.00 each. To calculate the approximate APR for the loan, follow these steps:

1. Find the total amount paid using the formula below. Note that the total amount paid includes a down payment, if one is made, and all the loan payments.

Formula	(Number of Payments × Payment Amount) + Down Payment = Total Amount Paid
Example	(12 × $66.00) + $100.00 = $892.00

2. Find the total finance charge using the formula below.

Formula	Total Amount Paid − Cash Price = Finance Charge
Example	$892.00 − $800.00 = $92.00

3. Find the APR using the formula below. Letters in the formula are explained below.

    n = Number of Payment Periods in One Year
    f = Finance Charge
    P = Principal of Loan
    N = Total Number of Payments to Repay the Loan

Formula	$\dfrac{2 \times n \times f}{P \times (N+1)} = APR$
Example	$\dfrac{2 \times 12 \times \$92.00}{\$700.00 \times (12+1)} = \dfrac{2{,}208}{9{,}100} = .2426 = 24.26\%$

Directions: Find the APR for the loans described below. Refer to the formulas and examples given on the previous page. You can use spreadsheet software or do the math manually. You may wish to access an APR calculator online and enter the data to check your calculations. The formula finds the approximate APR. So the answer you get from an APR calculator may be slightly different. Round your answers to two decimal places.

1. The Smiths are buying a new refrigerator. The cash price is $1,925.00. They will make a down payment of $125.00. The balance will be covered by an installment loan. The loan will be repaid in 24 monthly payments of $88.00. They have been quoted a loan interest rate of 8 percent. What is the annual percentage rate for the loan?

2. The Chin family is borrowing $5,000.00 to take a vacation to Europe. The personal loan will have payments of $325.00 per month for 18 months. There is no down payment. (Use the loan amount as the cash price in the formula.) What is the annual percentage rate of the loan?

3. Your family is considering buying a utility shed. The cash price is $2,410.00. You will make a down payment of 5 percent of the cash price. You will take out an installment loan to cover the remainder. You will make monthly payments of $85.00 for 36 months. What is the annual percentage rate of the loan?

EXERCISE 8-6   Loan Amortization

Directions: Use the loan amortization table that follows to answer the questions below.

1. What is the principal of the loan?

2. What is the loan interest rate?

3. How many monthly payments will be made to repay the loan?

4. For Payment No. 1, how much of the payment is applied to the loan principal? How much is applied to interest?

5. For Payment No. 15, how much of the payment is applied to the loan principal? How much is applied to interest?

6. For Payment No. 36, how much of the payment is applied to the loan principal? How much is applied to interest?

7. As more payments are made, what effect does this have on the principal and interest paid?

AMORTIZATION TABLE

Loan Amount	$25,000.00
Loan Term	3 Years
Loan Interest Rate	5%
Monthly Payments	$749.27

Payment No.	1	2	3	4	5	6	7	8	9	10	11	12
Payment Amt.	$749.27	$749.27	$749.27	$749.27	$749.27	$749.27	$749.27	$749.27	$749.27	$749.27	$749.27	$749.27
Principal Paid	$645.11	$647.79	$650.49	$653.20	$655.92	$658.66	$661.40	$664.16	$666.93	$669.70	$672.49	$675.30
Interest Paid	$104.17	$101.48	$98.78	$96.07	$93.35	$90.61	$87.87	$85.11	$82.35	$79.57	$76.78	$73.98
Total Int. Paid	$104.17	$205.65	$304.42	$400.49	$493.84	$584.46	$672.33	$757.44	$839.79	$919.36	$996.13	$1,070.11
Balance	$24,354.89	$23,707.10	$23,056.61	$22,403.40	$21,747.48	$21,088.82	$20,427.42	$19,763.26	$19,096.34	$18,426.63	$17,754.14	$17,078.84

Payment No.	13	14	15	16	17	18	19	20	21	22	23	24
Payment Amt.	$749.27	$749.27	$749.27	$749.27	$749.27	$749.27	$749.27	$749.27	$749.27	$749.27	$749.27	$749.27
Principal Paid	$678.11	$680.94	$683.77	$686.62	$689.48	$692.36	$695.24	$698.14	$701.05	$703.97	$706.90	$709.85
Interest Paid	$71.16	$68.34	$65.50	$62.65	$59.79	$56.92	$54.03	$51.13	$48.23	$45.30	$42.37	$39.43
Total Int. Paid	$1,141.27	$1,209.61	$1,275.11	$1,337.76	$1,397.55	$1,454.46	$1,508.49	$1,559.63	$1,607.85	$1,653.16	$1,695.53	$1,734.96
Balance	$16,400.73	$15,719.79	$15,036.02	$14,349.40	$13,659.91	$12,967.56	$12,272.32	$11,574.18	$10,873.13	$10,169.16	$9,462.26	$8,752.42

Payment No.	25	26	27	28	29	30	31	32	33	34	35	36
Payment Amt.	$749.27	$749.27	$749.27	$749.27	$749.27	$749.27	$749.27	$749.27	$749.27	$749.27	$749.27	$749.27
Principal Paid	$712.80	$715.77	$718.76	$721.75	$724.76	$727.78	$730.81	$733.86	$736.91	$739.98	$743.07	$746.16
Interest Paid	$36.47	$33.50	$30.52	$27.52	$24.51	$21.49	$18.46	$15.42	$12.36	$9.29	$6.21	$3.11
Total Int. Paid	$1,771.42	$1,804.92	$1,835.44	$1,862.96	$1,887.47	$1,908.97	$1,927.43	$1,942.85	$1,955.20	$1,964.49	$1,970.70	$1,973.81
Balance	$8,039.61	$7,323.84	$6,605.08	$5,883.33	$5,158.57	$4,430.79	$3,699.98	$2,966.13	$2,229.21	$1,489.23	$746.16	$0.00

EXERCISE 8-7   The Costs of Credit

Directions: Enrique is thinking about buying a large, flat-panel television. He will need to borrow money to make the purchase. Answer the following questions about his purchase.

1.   What steps can Enrique take to minimize his total costs when buying the television?

2.   What steps can Enrique take to minimize his total costs when choosing a source of credit?

3.   What steps can Enrique take to minimize his credit costs following the purchase?

EXERCISE 8-8   Living Arrangements

Directions: As you prepare for life after school, there are many things to consider. Answer the questions that follow based on your post-high school plans.

1.   What are your plans following high school (work, college, special programs, military, etc.)?

2.   What do you think your living arrangements will be after high school? What items will you need (personal items, furniture, clothing, etc.)?

3.   Describe your living habits, including your living area, your social life, and so on. What would it be like to live with you?

4. What qualities would you look for in a roommate to help ensure compatibility?

5. Assume you will be sharing an apartment with two other roommates. List five "house rules" for all roommates to follow. Consider shared responsibilities.

6. What types of expenses do you think you will have when living on your own?

7. Describe your future goals—relating to your job, where you will live, and so on—five years after school.

NAME _____

EXERCISE 8-9   Group Budget

Directions: Based on the information that follows, prepare a group budget for three roommates. You may want to refer to Figure 8-1.1 in your textbook.

Three roommates will share the cost of an apartment. Monthly rent is $750. Monthly utilities are estimated to be $120, including electricity, water, and trash pickup. Groceries are estimated to cost $300 per month. Internet service costs $120 per month, including phone and TV cable. Roommate #2 has a pet (deposit of $100). The security deposit is $150, and cleaning fees are $90. The estimated monthly cost of household supplies is $60.

Expense	Monthly Cost	Roommate #1	Roommate #2	Roommate #3
Rent				
Utilities				
Groceries				
Internet/phone/cable				
Security deposit				
Cleaning fees				
Household supplies				
Total shared costs				
Pet deposit				

CHAPTER 9
Credit Problems and Laws

EXERCISE 9-1   Review of Chapter Key Terms

Directions: Write the letter of the correct definition beside its corresponding term.

_____ 1. alternative dispute resolution

_____ 2. bankruptcy

_____ 3. bankruptcy fraud

_____ 4. Chapter 7 bankruptcy

_____ 5. Chapter 13 bankruptcy

_____ 6. Credit Card Act of 2009

_____ 7. credit card fraud

_____ 8. credit counseling

_____ 9. credit delinquency

_____ 10. credit repair

_____ 11. debt consolidation

_____ 12. discharge

_____ 13. Equal Credit Opportunity Act

_____ 14. equity loan

_____ 15. exemption

_____ 16. Fair Credit Billing Act

_____ 17. Fair Credit Reporting Act

_____ 18. Fair Debt Collection Practices Act

_____ 19. foreclosure

_____ 20. garnishment

_____ 21. loan modification

_____ 22. Truth-in-Lending Act

A. A law that grants consumers the right to know what is in their credit files

B. A scam in which a company claims to be able to "fix" a person's poor credit record

C. A law that protects consumers from discrimination in the granting or denying of credit

D. A legal process that allows part of an employee's paycheck to be withheld for payment of a debt

E. A method of settling a dispute using a neutral third party

F. Intentionally using someone's credit account to steal money or goods

G. A legal procedure to relieve a person of excessive debt

H. A law requiring lenders to fully inform consumers about the cost of credit

I. A type of bankruptcy that involves a repayment plan

J. The proces of getting one loan with a single monthly payment to pay off all debts

K. A new loan arrangement that allows you to make reduced payments, usually on a temporary basis

L. A type of bankruptcy in which an individual forfeits assets in exchange for the discharge of debts

M. The legal process of taking possession of a house when a borrower does not make mortgage payments as agreed

N. Comprehensive reform to credit card law to establish fair practices

O. Property that a debtor in a bankruptcy does not have to forfeit

P. Failure to pay debts as required by agreement or by law

Q. A second mortgage or debt secured with the equity in your home

R. A law that sets requirements for resolving billing disputes

S. A law prohibiting abusive practices by collection agencies

T. Abusing bankruptcy laws in a way that favors the debtor

U. A court order that pardons a debtor from paying debts

V. A service to help consumers manage credit

EXERCISE 9-2   True/False Questions

Directions: Write the letter "T" for a true statement or "F" for a false statement.

_____ **23.** Consumers should keep receipts, statements, and other records until they are sure a product will perform as promised.

_____ **24.** Credit card fraud is the responsibility of the credit card companies, and the cost is not paid by consumers.

_____ **25.** State and federal agencies provide useful information and assistance for consumers who are affected by fraud and identity theft.

_____ **26.** Debt problems will affect your credit score.

_____ **27.** Creditors cannot legally attempt to collect debts.

_____ **28.** Garnishment is a method used to collect payment on a delinquent debt.

_____ **29.** A creditor cannot repossess the collateral used as security for a secured loan.

_____ **30.** All telemarketing calls are considered to be telemarketing fraud.

_____ **31.** Data miners gather, publish, and sell information about consumers.

_____ **32.** One of the most common reasons for personal bankruptcy is excessive medical bills.

_____ **33.** When consumers have debt problems, their first consideration should be filing for bankruptcy.

_____ **34.** All types of bankruptcy give the debtor an automatic stay from actions of their creditors.

EXERCISE 9-3   Multiple Choice Questions

Directions: Write the letter of the correct answer in the space provided.

_____ **35.** Liquidation bankruptcy is also called (a) business bankruptcy, (b) Chapter 7, (b) Chapter 11, (c) Chapter 13

_____ **36.** Debtors who want to file Chapter 7 bankruptcy must meet (a) a means test, (b) all debt obligations, (c) loan repayments, (d) debt adjustment

_____ **37.** Which Act allows you to view your credit file? (a) Truth-in-Lending Act, (b) Credit Card Act of 2009, (c) Fair Credit Reporting Act, (d) Fair Credit Billing Act

_____ **38.** Which of the following types of alternative dispute resolution may be binding? (a) negotiation, (b) arbitration, (c) mediation, (d) all of the above

_____ **39.** Which of the following legal actions allows for a quick resolution? (a) small claims court, (b) class action lawsuit, (c) individual lawsuit, (d) all of the above

_____ **40.** Which of the following consumer advocacy groups publishes *Consumer Reports*? (a) FTC, (b) Consumers Union, (c) Consumer Federation of America, (d) BBB

_____ **41.** Which of the following is *not* a recommended method to prevent credit card fraud? (a) carry only the cards you need, (b) close inactive accounts, (c) keep old statements containing account numbers, (d) monitor your credit activity online

_____ **42.** Which of the following is *not* a common reason for bankruptcy? (a) excessive medical bills, (b) low income, (c) overspending, (d) losing a job

_____ **43.** You give up your credit cards and turn over your checkbook when using (a) debt consolidation, (b) equity loans, (c) debt management, (d) bankruptcy

_____ **44.** Which of the following laws limits credit cards issued to teens without a cosigner? (a) Truth-in-Lending Act, (b) Credit Card Act of 2009, (c) Fair Credit Billing Act, (d) Equal Credit Opportunity Act

EXERCISE 9-4   Building Communications Skills: Persuasive Speaking

Directions: Giving a speech to convince people of your point of view or to take a certain action can be very challenging. You must present the information in a clear manner and gain the listeners' trust. Select a topic for a persuasive speech. You might choose a topic that is in the news or one that relates to current events at your school. Have your teacher approve the topic and then complete the steps below.

1. Write a purpose statement that clearly states the action you want listeners to take or the point of view you want them to support after hearing your speech.

2. Conduct research to find information to include in your speech.

3. Consider the audience (your classmates) and what they will already know about the topic. Identify reasons they might resist supporting your point of view or taking the action you will suggest.

4. Write an outline of the speech. The speech should last about 10 minutes.

5. Prepare visual aids such as a poster or slides to use in giving the speech.

6. Practice giving the speech, staying within the time limit of 10 minutes.

7. Deliver the speech to your class or a group of classmates.

8. Evaluate your speech. How successful was it? Ask the listeners whether they were convinced to take the action or support the point of view you proposed in the speech.

EXERCISE 9-5   Building Math Skills: Computing Exemptions

Directions: Assume the current federal bankruptcy exemptions are listed at the left, and the state exemptions are listed at the right. The debtor may use the exemption table that best benefits him or her. For the two circumstances described below, compute the exemption amounts and decide which will be better for the debtor—the federal list or the state list.

LIST A. FEDERAL EXEMPTIONS

Homestead	$21,625
Motor vehicle	3,450
Household goods ($550 limit per single item)	11,525
Jewelry	1,450
Wild card (other property)	1,450
Tools of trade	2,175

LIST B. STATE EXEMPTIONS

Homestead	$25,000
Motor vehicle	1,500
Household goods ($1,000 limit per single item)	10,000
Jewelry	500
Wild card (other property)	100
Tools of trade	5,000

1. Jerry has the following assets: a house with equity of $15,000, a car with equity of $2,500, and household goods worth $6,000 (no single item over $400). He also has tools worth $5,800 that he needs for his business. What is the total amount of exemptions Jerry would be allowed using the federal list? The state list? Which list will be more favorable for him?

2. Wilma has the following assets: a house with equity of $14,250, a car with equity of $2,700, and household goods worth $9,000 (no single item over $400). She also has jewelry worth $1,100 and other property worth $900. She has no tools used for work. What is the total amount of exemptions Wilma would be allowed using the federal list? The state list? Which list will be more favorable for her?

EXERCISE 9-6   Careers in Law

To become a lawyer in most states, a person must have a bachelor's degree followed by three years of law school. To practice law, a candidate must also pass a bar exam (after graduating from law school). A bar exam is a lengthy test that determines whether a person is qualified to practice law in a certain area. Every state gives its own bar exam. Some lawyers specialize in consumer laws; others specialize in areas such as taxation, real estate, and family law. You can visit websites such as Lawyers.com to find out about the different types of lawyers.

Directions: Learn more about careers in law. Access the *Occupational Outlook Handbook* online. Search the site using the term *lawyer*. Then answer the questions below.

1.   Describe some typical tasks and responsibilities for a lawyer?

2.   What is the employment outlook for this type of career?

3.   What are the median annual wage and salary earnings for lawyers?

4.   Does a career as a lawyer appeal to you? Why or why not?

EXERCISE 9-7   Credit Problems

Directions: Read the following scenarios and describe how you would handle each situation.

1. Jim and Fran have decided to try to get help with their credit problems rather than file for bankruptcy. They want more time to pay off loans, and they have several credit card debts with high interest rates. What would you suggest?

2. Ramon is deeply in debt. He knows that he will not be able to pay all his debts. He wants to be fair to the creditors, but he also needs a fresh start. He has a good job with a steady income. Explain to him the differences between Chapter 7 and Chapter 13 bankruptcy. Which one do you think would be appropriate for Ramon?

3. Although Alicia is working two jobs, she is deep in debt. She has a very large medical bill (exceeding $400,000) as a result of an illness two years ago. She has run up charges on her credit cards trying to pay off her medical bill. Because of the high interest rate on her credit cards, she is making little progress in paying off all of her bills. What do you suggest?

EXERCISE 9-8   Dealing with Difficult People

Directions: Read the following situations, and write your responses.

Situation 1

You are in charge of a meeting. One person is constantly interrupting you and making comments that are inappropriate. The meeting is stalled and has turned into a complaint session. The agenda is no longer being followed. Write a paragraph about what you would do, including steps you would take to get the meeting back on track.

Situation 2

You are a member of a five-person team that is working on a school project. Your grade will be based on a presentation given by the team. One member of your team is not carrying her weight. She does not show up for team meetings and has not done work as assigned. When asked to help, she always has excuses. What would you do as an individual member of the team?

CHAPTER 10
Basics of Saving and Investing

EXERCISE 10-1   Review of Chapter Key Terms

Directions: Write the letter of the correct definition beside its corresponding term.

_____ 1.   bear market

_____ 2.   bond

_____ 3.   bull market

_____ 4.   contingencies

_____ 5.   diversification

_____ 6.   dollar-cost averaging

_____ 7.   emergency fund

_____ 8.   estate

_____ 9.   financial market

_____ 10. financial security

_____ 11. foundation

_____ 12. industry risk

_____ 13. inflation risk

_____ 14. investing

_____ 15. investment portfolio

_____ 16. investment tracking

_____ 17. liquidity

_____ 18. market timing

_____ 19. political risk

_____ 20. retirement

_____ 21. stock

_____ 22. stock risk

_____ 23. tax deferral

_____ 24. tax-exempt

A. Buying and selling stocks based on what the market is expected to do

B. Money set aside for unplanned expenses

C. Chance that the rate of inflation will be higher than your investment rate of return

D. A period of time, usually in later years, when you are not working but are able to meet your expenses through other income sources

E. Chance that activities or events affecting a company will change the value of an investment in that company

F. All that a person owns (assets), less debts owed, at the time of that person's death

G. Period in the stock market when prices are steadily decreasing

H. Not subject to taxation

I. A technique for making investment choices by following the prices of stocks over time

J. A debt instrument issued by a corporation or government

K. A fund or an organization established for the purpose of supporting an institution or a cause

L. A measure of how quickly an asset can be turned into cash

M. Unplanned or possible events

N. A strategy to earn more on your money than the rate of inflation

O. A postponement of taxes to be paid

P. A place where investments are bought and sold

Q. Holding a variety of investments to reduce overall risk

R. The ability to meet current and future needs while living comfortably

S. Chance that factors affecting an industry as a whole will negatively affect the value of an investment

T. Chance that a political event will affect the value of an investment

U. Investing the same amount of money on a regular basis regardless of market conditions

V. Ownership interest in a publicly held company

W. Period in the stock market when prices are steadily increasing

X. A collection of assets that provides diversification

EXERCISE 10-2   True/False Questions

Directions: Write the letter "T" for a true statement or "F" for a false statement.

_____ 25. Savings and investing are related because it is the setting aside of money that provides funds for investing.

_____ 26. Most investments that are considered long-term are designed to stay ahead of inflation.

_____ 27. Contingency planning is considered a medium- or long-term goal.

_____ 28. For most people, financial security is not something they should consider until middle age or later.

_____ 29. You should start thinking about retirement when you begin your first career.

_____ 30. A savings account is considered to be a risk-free choice.

_____ 31. All stocks increase in value over time.

_____ 32. Tax deferral allows your investment to grow for years without being taxed.

_____ 33. An employer money match is not a good idea because the employer has control over your retirement account.

_____ 34. A systematic saving and investing plan is designed for growth in the long run, not for short-term results.

_____ 35. Investors should consider the economy when forming an investment strategy.

_____ 36. An economic decline is a good time to sell stocks because prices are falling.

EXERCISE 10-3   Multiple Choice Questions

Directions: Write the letter of the correct answer in the space provided.

_____ 37. The emphasis of savings is on (a) growth over time, (b) safety of principal, (c) risky investments, (d) none of the above

_____ 38. Which of the following is a risk-free investment? (a) stocks, (b) savings bonds, (c) corporate bonds, (d) real estate

_____ 39. The payment made to a stockholder when a corporation makes a profit is called a(n) (a) interest payment, (b) gain on principal, (c) return on investment, (d) dividend

_____ 40. If employees of a company go on strike, this is an example of (a) stock risk, (b) industry risk, (c) political risk, (d) inflation risk

_____ 41. When prices are rising rapidly, this can lead to which type of risk? (a) stock risk, (b) industry risk, (c) political risk, (d) inflation risk

_____ 42. An investment that will *not* be taxed until a later time is (a) tax-deferred, (b) tax-exempt, (c) nontaxable, (d) tax-free

_____ 43. When investors sell stocks that have increased in value, this is an example of (a) diversification, (b) systematic investing, (c) profit-taking, (d) dollar-cost averaging

_____ 44. To calculate the return on investment (ROI), divide the amount you gained on the investment by the (a) dividends received, (b) taxes paid, (c) amount you invested, (d) none of the above

_____ 45. Which of the following is an example of a tax-exempt investment? (a) stocks, (b) savings bonds, (c) corporate bonds, (d) savings accounts

_____ 46. A diversified investment portfolio will most likely contain (a) stocks, (b) bonds, (c) mutual funds, (d) all of the above

EXERCISE 10-4   Building Communications Skills: Good News Messages

The letter that follows is an example of a good news message. The writer states the main point of the message in the first paragraph. Then the writer gives details in the second paragraph. Finally, the writer closes the message cordially to build goodwill.

Jackson Motors
1501 Silver Spring Drive
Milwaukee, WI 53209-1501

January 31, 20--

Ms. Janice LaCrosse
9033 Greenfield Avenue
Milwaukee, WI 53214-9033

Dear Ms. LaCrosse

Your letter requesting a repair to your car arrived yesterday. We will be happy to make the repair you requested. We have had other reports of similar problems, and we believe that you are right. The part that is damaged was likely defective.

Please call us at 414-555-0134 to let us know when you can bring in your car. The work can be completed within a couple of hours. We will provide a loaner vehicle for you to use during this time if you need one.

Thank you for trusting us with your car. Your business is important to us. If you have any questions regarding the repair, please call me.

Sincerely

Joe Chou

Joe Chou
Manager

Directions: Write a good news letter to someone. Think of a situation in which you can give a reader good news. Example situations are provided below. Use one of these or choose another situation. In the first paragraph, state the good news clearly. In the second paragraph, give supporting details. In the third paragraph, close the message and build goodwill. Use the letter on the previous page as an example for format and style. Proofread the letter carefully and correct all errors.

- The reader is being hired for a job that he or she interviewed for recently.

- The reader's request for credit has been granted.

- The reader's hotel reservation is confirmed, and she or he has been upgraded to a better room at no additional charge.

EXERCISE 10-5   Building Math Skills: Return on Investment

Example 1 (Gain in Principal)

Bill bought 40 shares of stock at $22.15 per share. A year later, he sold them for $28.90 a share. How much did he make in dollars, and what was his return on investment (ROI)?

Solution:
$40 \times \$22.15 = \$886.00$ purchase price
$40 \times \$28.90 = \$1,156.00$ sale price

$\$1,156.00 - \$886.00 = \$270.00$ profit in dollars
$\$270.00/\$886.00 = 0.304 = 30\%$ ROI

Example 2 (Gain in Dividends)

Jan bought 30 shares of stock at $25.00 per share. The company paid dividends of $1.00 per share last year. How much did she make in dollars, and what was her ROI?

Solution:
$30 \times \$25.00 = \$750.00$ purchase price
$30 \times \$1.00 = \$30.00$ profit in dividends
$\$30.00/\$750.00 = 0.04 = 4\%$ ROI

Note: This ROI is for comparison only. It is not real because the stock was not sold.

Example 3 (Gain in Principal and Dividends)

Jack bought 50 shares of stock at $18.22 per share. That year, he received total dividends of $72.88. At the end of the year, his stock was valued at $19.11 per share. What is his ROI?

Solution:
$50 \times \$18.22 = \$911.00$ purchase price
$50 \times \$19.11 = \$955.50$ value at end of year
$\$955.50 - \$911.00 = \$44.50$ gain in value
$\$44.50 + \$72.88 = \$117.38$ total profit
$\$117.38/\$911.00 = 0.128 = 13\%$ ROI

Note: This ROI is for comparison only. It is not real because the stock was not sold.

Directions: Compute the ROI for the following investments. Round your answers to the nearest percent.

1. Maurice bought 25 shares of stock at $9.85 per share and sold them for $11.22 per share. What was his ROI?

2. Jill bought 100 shares of stock at $12.44 per share and sold them for $13.11 per share. What was her ROI?

3. Patrick bought 30 shares of stock at $16.49 per share. He received dividends of $.75 per share for 1 year. What is his ROI?

4. Janice bought 40 shares of stock at $31.82 per share. She received dividends of $1.11 per share for 1 year. What is her ROI?

5. Chiko bought 75 shares of stock at $19.58 per share. She received dividends of $73.42 during the year. At the end of the year, her stock was valued at $22.14. What is her ROI?

6. Tomas bought 25 shares of stock at $59.25 per share. He received dividends of $74.06 during the year. At the end of the year, his stock was valued at $61.50. What is his ROI?

EXERCISE 10-6   Dollar-Cost Averaging

Dollar-cost averaging can be a successful investment strategy for some people. Using this strategy, a person saves and invests the same amount of money on a regular basis, such as monthly. The amount is invested regardless of whether prices are high or low.

Directions:

1. Assume you use the dollar-cost averaging investment strategy. You invest up to $200 on the first day of each month in a balanced mutual fund. Buying shares in the mutual fund provides some diversification and lowers your risk.

2. The table below shows the date of investment and the amount you had available to invest. It also shows the price of a share in the mutual fund on that date. Complete the table by filling in the number of shares you were able to buy and the actual amount paid. You will buy as many shares as you can purchase for $200 or less. Any money left over from the $200 will be placed in your savings account. The first transaction has been completed as an example.

Date	Money Available to Invest	Share Price	Shares Bought	Amount Paid
January 1	$200.00	$49.00	4	$196.00
February 1	$200.00	$46.50		
March 1	$200.00	$48.00		
April 1	$200.00	$49.75		
May 1	$200.00	$50.00		
June 1	$200.00	$52.00		
July 1	$200.00	$53.00		
August 1	$200.00	$55.00		
September 1	$200.00	$50.00		
October 1	$200.00	$48.00		
November 1	$200.00	$47.00		
December 1	$200.00	$50.00		

3. After your December 1 purchase, what is the average share price you paid? Round to the nearest cent.

4. After your December 1 purchase, how many shares do you have? What is the average cost per share?

5. On December 20, you sold all your shares for $53.00 per share. What is your ROI? Round to the nearest percent.

6. How much money did you have left over to put in your savings account?

EXERCISE 10-7   Investment Strategies

Directions: Work with a classmate to complete this activity. Read each of the following scenarios and then describe the saving and investing strategy you would recommend. Give reasons why you selected this strategy.

Scenario A

Ben Fong has saved $1,000. Currently, the money is earning 0.5 percent interest in a checking account. Ben works part time and goes to high school. He plans to start college in four or five years. Ben does not have any other savings or investments.

Scenario B

Bill and Barbara Wilson are a married couple. Both of them are working, and they pay taxes at a high rate (35 percent). They have saved $5,000 and wish to invest it for the future. They have other savings and retirement plans, including both low-risk and high-risk investments.

Scenario C

Gloria Vega just inherited $1,500 from her uncle. She is single, 25 years old, and living with her parents. Gloria works full time while attending college part time. She has a savings account totaling $2,500 and no investments.

NAME _____

EXERCISE 10-8   Portfolio Diversification

An investment portfolio is a group of assets, such as certificates of deposit, stocks, and bonds. The portfolio should be diversified to lower risk. Investment choices will vary based on the person's age, income, family situation, goals, and attitude toward risk. They will also vary depending on the amount of money to be invested. In this activity, you will think about how to select types of investments for a diversified portfolio.

Assume that you are 28 years old. You have completed college and have a job that pays $40,000 a year. You have no debt and no dependents that you help support. You have savings of $30,000. You have decided to create a diversified investment portfolio.

Directions: Answer the following questions to help you think about how to structure your portfolio. Refer to Figure 10-3.2 in your textbook to see the different portfolio categories and types of investments. Select amounts for each category based on your attitude toward investing and your risk comfort level.

1. What percentage of your savings will you place in the foundation portion of the portfolio? What will this amount be in dollars? What types of investments will you include in this portion of the portfolio?

2. What percentage of your savings will you place in the conservative investments portion of the portfolio? What will this amount be in dollars? What types of investments will you include in this portion of the portfolio?

3. What percentage of your savings will you place in the growth investments portion of the portfolio? What will this amount be in dollars? What types of investments will you include in this portion of the portfolio?

4. What percentage of your savings will you place in the speculative investments portion of the portfolio? What will this amount be in dollars? What types of investments will you include in this portion of the portfolio?

5. Develop a systematic investing strategy. What amount of money will you plan to invest each coming month or year to help build your portfolio?

6. What long-term goals do you want to achieve? How will this affect the types of investments you choose?

CHAPTER 11
Saving and Investing Options

EXERCISE 11-1   Review of Chapter Key Terms

Directions: Write the letter of the correct definition beside its corresponding term.

_____ 1. 401(k) plan

_____ 2. 403(b) plan

_____ 3. annuity

_____ 4. asset allocation

_____ 5. callable bond

_____ 6. clearing account

_____ 7. collectibles

_____ 8. commodity

_____ 9. common stock

_____ 10. coupon rate

_____ 11. direct investing

_____ 12. discount bond

_____ 13. franchise

_____ 14. futures contract

_____ 15. gems

_____ 16. illiquid

_____ 17. indirect investing

_____ 18. Keogh account

_____ 19. mutual fund

_____ 20. precious metals

_____ 21. preferred stock

_____ 22. premium bond

_____ 23. rollover

_____ 24. Roth IRA

_____ 25. zero coupon bond

A. A bond that is sold for more than its face value

B. An agreement to buy or sell a specific commodity at a set price on a set date in the future

C. Rare, valuable objects, such as fine art, coins and books

D. Stock that pays variable dividends and gives voting rights

E. Tax-deferred retirement plan funded by employees of profit-seeking businesses

F. Buying shares of a mutual fund instead of buying individual shares of stock in various companies

G. A contract purchased from an insurance company that guarantees a series of regular payments for a set time

H. A professionally managed group of investments bought using a pool of money from many investors

I. Not convertible to cash quickly or without a penalty

J. An item that has the same value across the market with little or no difference in quality among producers

K. The process of moving a retirement account balance to another qualified account without incurring a tax penalty

L. Choosing a combination of funds within a single mutual fund company

M. Stock that guarantees fixed dividends but has no voting rights

N. A discount corporate bond that does not pay semiannual interest

O. An account used to buy and sell investments

P. A bond that is sold for less than its face value

Q. Rare metals, which are usually natural substances

R. Buying stocks directly from companies and holding them

S. The fixed rate of interest paid semiannually on a bond

T. Natural, precious stones such as diamonds

U. An individual retirement account in which contributions are taxed, but earnings are not

V. A bond with a clause that allows the issuer to repay the bond early

W. Tax-deferred retirement plan for self-employed professionals

X. Tax-deferred reteirement plan funded by employees of government and nonprofit organizations

Y. Contract that gives you the right to sell a company's products

EXERCISE 11-2　True/False Questions

Directions: Write the letter "T" for a true statement or "F" for a false statement.

_____ **26.** Savings should be in a form that is liquid.

_____ **27.** A savings account typically pays a low rate because it is not insured.

_____ **28.** Brokerage accounts are usually insured with the FDIC.

_____ **29.** An early withdrawal penalty can result in a loss of interest, but it cannot affect your principal.

_____ **30.** When a CD is pledged to secure a loan, you can generally get a lower rate of interest on that loan.

_____ **31.** A good way to save money is to purchase a permanent life insurance policy.

_____ **32.** All bonds sell at face value.

_____ **33.** Treasury bills are guaranteed to keep pace with the rate of inflation.

_____ **34.** Municipal bonds are issued by state governments.

_____ **35.** A callable bond can be exchanged for shares of stock at the option of the bond holder.

_____ **36.** Dividend earnings on corporate stock are not subject to federal income tax.

_____ **37.** Buying mutual funds is a form of direct investing.

_____ **38.** Owning your own home is considered a very good tax shelter.

EXERCISE 11-3　Multiple Choice Questions

Directions: Write the letter of the correct answer in the space provided.

_____ **39.** Which of the following retirement accounts provides tax-free earnings? (a) traditional IRA, (b) Roth IRA, (c) spousal IRA, (d) all of the above

_____ **40.** Which of the following retirement plans pays benefits according to an employee's highest salary earned while working? (a) defined-benefit plan, (b) defined-contribution plan, (c) 401(k) plan, (d) annuity plan

_____ **41.** Which of the following methods of investing is the riskiest? (a) buying mutual funds, (b) buying corporate bonds, (c) buying common stock, (d) buying an annuity

_____ **42.** Which of the following would be considered a speculative investment? (a) stocks, (b) vacant lot, (c) rental property, (d) corporate bonds

_____ **43.** When you borrow against a CD or other account, it is known as what? (a) early withdrawal, (b) inflation risk, (c) pledging, (d) a jumbo CD

_____ **44.** Which of the following investments is *not* taxable if used for education purposes? (a) Treasury bonds, (b) Treasury bills, (c) TIPS, (d) I bonds

_____ **45.** Which of following type of bond is a debt obligation for a city, county, or state? (a) EE bond, (b) municipal bond, (c) corporate bond, (d) I bond

_____ **46.** Which of the following types of bonds is likely to be more attractive to investors? (a) callable bonds, (b) zero coupon bonds, (c) convertible bonds, (d) all of the above

_____ **47.** Which type of mutual fund aims to produce steady and reliable dividend and interest payments for investors? (a) balanced fund, (b) global fund, (c) growth fund, (d) income fund

_____ **48.** Which of the following investments increases with inflation and decreases with deflation? (a) TIPS, (b) EE bonds, (c) Treasury bonds, (d) I bonds

EXERCISE 11-4   Building Communications Skills: Bad News Messages

The letter that follows is an example of a bad news message. In the first paragraph, the writer explains the situation and builds trust so that the reader will agree with the decision and remain a customer. The writer gently and logically leads the reader to the decision or bad news, while maintaining goodwill.

Jackson Motors
1501 Silver Spring Drive
Milwaukee, WI 53209-1501

January 31, 20--

Ms. Janice LaCrosse
9033 Greenfield Avenue
Milwaukee, WI 53214-9033

Dear Ms. LaCrosse

Thank you for your letter of January 26. We have considered the possible causes of the repairs that need to be made to your car. You have reported that the engine light comes on and off sporadically and that there is a sloshing sound in your dashboard.

Your car should have immediate attention. We think that the problem is probably in the cooling system. With a diagnostic test, we will know for sure. At 42,000 miles, your car may have many parts that are beginning to wear out and need replacing. Your car can probably be repaired effectively in a day. When a car is driven beyond the warranty period, some parts are still under warranty. That includes many engine and body parts. The cooling system, however, is designed to be serviced and repaired at regular intervals. We have calculated that the work will take about four hours. The parts will cost approximately $120. We estimate that the total cost for the repair will be $300 or less.

Please call us at 414-555-0134 to set up an appointment to fix the problems that are occurring with your car. We will provide a loaner car at no charge to you for the day when your car is in the shop.

Sincerely

Joe Chou

Joe Chou
Manager

Directions: Write a bad news letter to someone. Think of a situation in which you will give a reader bad news. Example situations are provided below. Use one of these or choose another situation. In the first paragraph, mention the situation and state that you have received the reader's request or complaint. In the second paragraph, give supporting details and the decision or bad news. In the third paragraph, close the message and build goodwill. Use the letter on the previous page as an example for format and style. Proofread the letter carefully and correct all errors.

- You cannot ship the reader's order of backyard bricks for a week due to shortage problems with a supplier. The customer wanted the bricks to start work on a project in three days.

- A request for a credit increase has been denied at this time because the reader has too many bank credit cards with high balances. You want to keep the reader as a customer because his or her payments have always been on time.

- The flight the reader booked six months ago is being canceled, and the airline will no longer be flying to that destination. A refund will be issued. There are flights with other airlines (which cost more) that are available.

EXERCISE 11-5   Building Math Skills: Bond Profits

Directions: Complete the following problems to find profits for bonds. Review Figure 11-1.2 in the textbook if needed.

1. Timothy bought a bond with a face value of $1,000. The bond term is 1 year. He bought the bond at a 5 percent discount from the face value. The bond pays 5 percent annual interest, and Timothy will receive two semiannual payments. When the bond is redeemed at maturity, what will be the total return (profit) in dollars? What will be the total return on investment? (Remember that return on investment is given as a percentage.)

2. Alejandro bought a bond with a face value of $5,000. The term of the bond is 2 years. He bought the bond at a 4 percent discount from the face value. The bond pays 4 percent annual interest, and Alejandro will receive four semiannual payments. When the bond is redeemed at maturity, what will be the total return in dollars? What will be the total return on investment?

3. Chelsea bought a bond with a face value of $5,000. The bond has a term of 4 years. Chelsea bought the bond at a 3 percent discount from the face value. The bond pays 3 percent annual interest, and Chelsea will receive eight semiannual payments. When the bond is redeemed at maturity, what will be the total return in dollars? What will be the total return on investment?

EXERCISE 11-6   Careers in Real Estate

Many people are interested in owning, managing, or selling real estate. Some jobs in this career area pay commissions only. Others are based on profits at sale. Some real estate career areas that might interest you are listed below.

CAREER	DESCRIPTION
Real estate sales associate	• Assists buyers and sellers in the buying or selling of real estate • Helps locate properties • Works with buyers to help them qualify for mortgage loans • Prepares documents to make offers and follows through with sales and closings • Works with lenders, title companies, inspectors, and appraisers • Works on commission sales
Real estate broker	• Works in the buying and selling of real estate • Supervises real estate sales associates and is responsible for transactions for the real estate office • Earns a percentage of commissions from sales associates as well as own commissions for selling
Real estate office manager	• Maintains the real estate office • Schedules desk/floor duty and coordinates meetings • Facilitates deposits and keeps records of completed and pending sales • Works for a salary
Property manager	• Manages income properties for owners • Coordinates maintenance and repairs • Collects rent, keeps good records, and reports to owners • Works for a percentage of rents collected
Real estate appraiser	• Determines the market value of real estate • Does assessments and comparisons for market analysis • Works for a flat fee for each appraisal
Real estate mortgage broker	• Works with buyers to help them qualify for mortgage loans • Coordinates paperwork for underwriters and supervises the loan process • Works for mortgage lending fees paid by mortgage companies
Real estate inspector	• Inspects property that is being sold to be sure it is in good repair • Checks roof, electrical, plumbing, understructure, drainage, heating, and all aspects of a property's condition • Works for a flat fee for each inspection
Real estate investor	• Buys real estate for personal and income purposes • Is responsible for repairs and upkeep • Makes profits from rental income and from sales • May buy fixer-uppers, make repairs, and resell the properties

Directions: Learn more about one career related to real estate. Access the *Occupational Outlook Handbook* online. Search the site using the term *real estate*. Choose links from the search results that will take you to job information. Then answer the questions below.

1. What is the employment outlook for this type of career?

2. What type of education and qualifications are required for this job?

3. What are the median annual wage and salary earnings for the job?

4. Does this job appeal to you? Why or why not?

EXERCISE 11-7   High-Risk Investment Choices

Directions: Assume that you are financially secure. You have money to invest in a high-risk option in the hope of making a high return. Read the three descriptions of investment options below. Under the "Your Choice" heading, explain which option you would choose and why. Explain what you would do, whom you would talk to, or how you would proceed with making the investment.

Option A

A friend wants to open her own small business. She has a good idea for a new product but needs financial backing. Because she has no credit established and no collateral, the bank is unwilling to lend her money. She is asking you to become an investor and to contribute $10,000 in exchange for a share of the profits.

Option B

A friend has collected coins for many years. He has a nice collection that has been appraised at more than $5,000. You want to buy some type of collectibles. What type would you be interested in investing in? Your friend does not want to sell his coin collection, but he is willing to help you get started.

Option C

You are aware of a house that you could buy for rental property. The house is in a neighborhood where home prices have been rising steadily for the past several years. The house and lawn have been neglected. You think that routine care and a few minor repairs could make the property more valuable. Because it needs some repairs and maintenance, you could buy the house at a low price.

Your Choice

EXERCISE 11-8   Rental Property Return on Investment

Directions: Read the following information about real estate investing and answer the questions that follow.

Buying rental property is an investment option that carries a higher risk than some other options. However, the returns can be good. Assume you have purchased a single-family home that you intend to rent for $750 per month. You will have the following expenses:

- Monthly mortgage $390
- Monthly insurance $60
- Semiannual property taxes $340
- Repairs (yearly estimate) $500
- Monthly lawn care or snow removal $100

1.   Calculate the total yearly expenses you will have for the rental property.

2.   Calculate the total rent you will receive in a year. Assume the house is rented for the full 12 months per year.

3.   What is your return on investment for the property?

4. Some of your expenses have increased, as shown below. Calculate the total yearly expenses you will have for the rental property after the cost increases.

- Monthly insurance $70
- Semiannual property taxes $380
- Monthly lawn care or snow removal $115

5. What is the new return on investment for the property?

6. What could you do to increase your return on investment?

7. Explain why a positive cash flow is important to owners of rental property.

CHAPTER 12
Buying and Selling Investments

EXERCISE 12-1   Review of Chapter Key Terms

Directions: Write the letter of the correct definition beside its corresponding term.

_____	1.	annual report
_____	2.	auction market
_____	3.	buy and hold
_____	4.	buying on margin
_____	5.	discount broker
_____	6.	discretionary order
_____	7.	FINRA
_____	8.	limit order
_____	9.	market order
_____	10.	NCUA
_____	11.	odd lot
_____	12.	oversight
_____	13.	over-the-counter market
_____	14.	primary market
_____	15.	round lot
_____	16.	Sarbanes-Oxley
_____	17.	SEC
_____	18.	secondary market
_____	19.	securities exchange
_____	20.	selling short
_____	21.	stock dividend
_____	22.	stock split
_____	23.	stock turning
_____	24.	stop order
_____	25.	Wall Street Reform Act

A. Exactly 100 shares or multiples of 100 shares of stock

B. An order to buy or sell stock that allows the broker to get the best possible price

C. Request to sell stock when it reaches a certain price

D. Borrowing money from your broker to buy stock

E. Fewer than 100 shares of stock

F. Private organization that regulates firms selling securities in the United States

G. Request to buy or sell stock at a specific price

H. A company's report to shareholders about the financial position of the company

I. Network of dealers and brokers who buy and sell stocks and other securities that are not listed on a securities exchange

J. A place where brokers buy and sell securities for their clients

K. Plan to purchase and keep stock for the long term

L. A qualified stockbroker who buys and sells securities at a reduced commission but offers no advice

M. The issuance of more stock to current stockholders in some proportion to the stock they already own

N. Market in which stock is sold to the highest bidder

O. Primary overseer of the U.S. securities market

P. Law that is designed to create and maintain a stable financial system

Q. Request to buy or sell stock at the current market price

R. Financial market in which new issues of securities are sold

S. Financial market in which previously issued securities are bought and sold

T. Selling stock that has been borrowed from a broker and replacing it at a later date

U. Dividend paid in the form of new shares of stock

V. A regulatory agency's supervision of activities to ensure that investors' rights are protected

W. Federal agency that charters and supervises credit unions

X. Making regular and systematic changes in stock ownership based on trends in the economy

Y. Law that sets stronger standards for public companies and accounting firms regarding financial reporting of operations

Directions: Write the letter "T" for a true statement or "F" for a false statement.

_____ **26.** *Forbes* is an example of a business magazine that covers investment topics.

_____ **27.** A stockbroker does not typically charge a fee for giving investment advice or for making a sale or purchase transaction for an investor.

_____ **28.** Online brokerage firms typically charge lower fees, generally because they give the least amount of service.

_____ **29.** It is a good idea to check the background of a broker at the FINRA website.

_____ **30.** An initial public offering (IPO) is available for purchase in the secondary market.

_____ **31.** New security issues are offered through securities exchanges.

_____ **32.** Direct investing is less expensive than buying stocks at securities exchanges because there are no broker fees involved.

_____ **33.** Stock splits involve brokerage fees, and they are taxable income.

_____ **34.** A request to buy or sell stock is called an "order."

_____ **35.** A discretionary order is a request to buy or sell at a specific price.

_____ **36.** Selling short involves using leverage, or borrowing money in the form of stock.

_____ **37.** You can save money by using a discount broker to buy and sell stocks.

EXERCISE 12-3   Multiple Choice Questions

Directions: Write the letter of the correct answer in the space provided.

_____ **38.** Which of the following agencies was created to promote public confidence in the banking system? (a) SEC, (b) FDIC, (c) NCUA, (d) OCC

_____ **39.** Which of the following agencies is responsible for enforcing securities laws? (a) FDIC, (b) OTS, (c) SEC, (d) PBGC

_____ **40.** Which of the following is an investor newsletter? (a) *Standard and Poor's*, (b) *Wall Street Journal*, (c) *Fortune*, (d) *BusinessWeek*

_____ **41.** Which of the following types of data would *not* be found in an annual report? (a) dividends paid, (b) profits made, (c) future plans, (d) all of the above would be included in an annual report

_____ **42.** Which of the following is an auction market? (a) AMEX, (b) NYSE, (c) both of the above, (d) none of the above

_____ **43.** An electronic marketplace for over-the-counter stocks is called? (a) AMEX, (b) NYSE, (c) FINRA, (d) NASDAQ

_____ **44.** Which of the following is *not* considered a form of reinvesting? (a) cash dividends, (b) stock dividends, (c) stock splits, (d) all of the above are forms of reinvesting

_____ **45.** Receiving two shares of stock for each share you currently own is called a(n) (a) stock dividend, (b) cash dividend, (c) stock split, (d) auction market

_____ **46.** The first step in buying securities is to (a) place a transaction, (c) call a stockbroker, (c) purchase stock, (d) set up an account

_____ **47.** When you direct your stockbroker to sell stock when it reaches a certain price, you are making a _____ order. (a) limit order, (b) stop order, (c) market order, (d) discretionary order

EXERCISE 12-4   Building Communications Skills: Persuasive Messages

The letter that follows is an example of a persuasive message. The writer wants to convince the reader to do something. A persuasive message must present points in a logical order and offer evidence to persuade the reader.

Jackson Motors
1501 Silver Spring Drive
Milwaukee, WI 53209-1501

April 30, 20--

Ms. Janice LaCrosse
9033 Greenfield Avenue
Milwaukee, WI 53214-9033

Dear Ms. LaCrosse

Thank you for letting us know about the problems with your service call last week. We want to provide high-quality service in all areas of our business. To apologize for your inconvenience, we would like to handle your next service need in a special way.

Your car will need its 50,000-mile checkup work next month. Please allow us to do that work for you at no cost for our labor. The service will include tire rotation; lube, oil, and filter; brake fluid; transmission check; and the full bumper-to-bumper safety check. A coupon that you can redeem for this offer is enclosed.

Ms. LaCrosse, we value you as a customer. You bought your car from us, and you have trusted us to work on it in the past. Our work and parts are fully guaranteed. Please allow us to win your confidence by accepting our offer of free labor on your next service visit.

Sincerely

Joe Chou

Joe Chou
Manager

Enclosure

Directions: Write a persuasive letter to someone. Think of a situation in which you want to persuade the reader to take some action or agree to some plan. Example situations are provided below. Use one of these or choose another situation. Use the letter on the previous page as an example for format and style. Proofread the letter carefully and correct all errors.

- Acknowledge that your company made an error on the reader's bill, and indicate that it will be corrected immediately. Enclose a coupon for a 40 percent savings on any item purchased in the store.

- Apologize for the actions of a rude employee. The employee continued talking on the phone in what appeared to be a private conversation rather than answering the questions of a customer in the store. Enclose a $10 coupon to be used in the future.

- Respond to a customer satisfaction survey in which the customer reported being dissatisfied with the quality of the food and the slow service in a restaurant. Enclose a coupon for a free meal of the customer's choice.

EXERCISE 12-5   Building Math Skills: Buying on Margin

Directions:

1. Luc Do purchased stocks for $6,000. He paid $4,000 in cash and borrowed $2,000 from the brokerage firm. He bought 100 shares at $60.00 per share ($6,000 total). The loan has an annual interest rate of 8 percent. Six months later, Luc Do sold the stock for $65 per share. He paid a commission of $120 and repaid the loan. What is his net profit? For help in completing this problem, review Figure 12-2.2 in your textbook, which illustrates buying on margin.

2. Carolyn bought 200 shares of stock at $30.00 per share ($6,000 total). She paid $3,000 in cash and borrowed $3,000 from the brokerage firm. The loan has an annual interest rate of 5 percent. Six months later, she sold the stock for $40 per share. Carolyn paid a commission of $120 and repaid the loan. What is her net profit?

3. Nathan bought 200 shares of stock at $40 per share ($8,000 total). He paid $5,000 in cash and borrowed $3,000 from the brokerage firm. The loan has an annual interest rate of 6 percent. Six months later, the stock's current price is $38 per share. If Nathan sells now, he will pay a commission of $160 and will have to repay the loan. If he sells now, how much will he lose?

EXERCISE 12-6   Careers with the SEC

The SEC (U.S. Securities and Exchange Commission) offers career opportunities related to law, finance, information technology, and other areas. In this exercise, you will learn about some of the jobs offered and how to apply for those jobs.

Directions:

1.   Access the Internet and visit the SEC website (www.sec.gov).

2.   On the SEC website, click the *Jobs* link. A screen with information about jobs at the SEC will appear, similar to the one shown below.

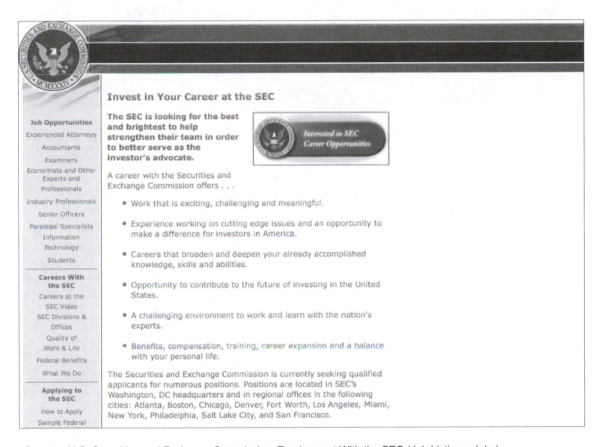

Source: U.S. Securities and Exchange Commission, Employment With the SEC (Job Listings–Jobs), http://www.sec.gov/jobs.shtml (accessed November 15, 2010).

3.   List the various job opportunities you find at the SEC website.

4. Click the link for one of the job areas that interests you and read more about it. Describe one specific job listed for that job area.

5. Click the link that leads to information about applying for a job with the SEC. List the main steps given for the application process.

6. Click on the link for *Federal Benefits*. What benefits do SEC employees receive?

7. Would a career with the SEC interest you? Why or why not?

EXERCISE 12-7   Investment Blogs

A blog (a shortened form of *weblog*) is an online place where you can find short articles or comments on a particular subject area. Blogs usually include text messages. However, some blogs contain photos, videos, or sound. Blogs may read like a journal, and they are often shown with the most recent entry first. A blog may be posted by one individual. Some blogs are posted by companies or organizations. Several people may write the postings in a blog. Access to many blogs is free. Some blogs charge a fee for access.

Many blogs that deal with investing are available. Seeking Alpha is a network of blogs with articles posted by people such as portfolio managers, research analysts, and financial advisers. Investors may find the articles and comments posted on blogs helpful when making investment decisions. They should be careful, however, about accepting the information posted on all blogs. Some blogs contain comments based on the investing strategy and ideas of one individual. This individual may or may not be qualified to give investing advice. Consider the source of the posting when deciding on its value. Is the article written by a person trained to give investing advice? Are sources listed so facts can be checked? Does the advice make sense when you compare it to the advice given in other articles you have read? Answering these questions can help you examine the value of a blog posting.

Directions: Access the Internet and key the term *investment blog* into a search engine. Then answer the questions below.

1.   Click several of the links in the search results to find at least three investment blogs that you think would be of value to investors. List the blog names and web addresses.

2.   Read a posting (an article) on one of the investment blogs. Give the title of the entry and write a summary of its contents. Do you think this posting was helpful? Why or why not?

EXERCISE 12-8   Investment Strategies

When evaluating stock investments, investors often classify stocks into different categories, as described below. Which category is best for you will depend on how much risk you are willing to assume for a chance to earn higher returns on your investments. Most investors buy stocks in several of these categories to diversify their risk.

STOCK DESCRIPTIONS

Blue-Chip Stock	A blue-chip stock is issued by a company that has been around for a long time and is a solid company. These stocks are considered safe investments. Examples are General Electric and McDonald's.
Income Stock	An income stock pays higher-than-average dividends. It is a source of steady, predictable income. Stocks issued by gas and utility companies are often considered income stocks; they are usually preferred stock. As such, the price is higher than for common stock.
Growth Stock	A growth stock is issued by a company that is young but has potential to grow over time. Investors are not seeking dividends but rather gains in stock values. These stocks are sometimes risky, but they can be part of a long-term investing strategy.
Cyclical Stock	A cyclical stock does well in a good economy but drops in value during bad economic times. If you believe the economy is about to do well, these stocks represent a good choice.
Defensive Stock	A defensive stock remains stable when the economy does poorly. It is a good, solid performer that barely reacts to economic conditions. These stocks represent goods and services that must be bought and sold regardless of the economy (such as groceries and utilities).
Large-Cap Stock	A large-cap stock is issued by a very large company with a lot of stock outstanding. These companies are considered safe (and their stock is often blue-chip stock as well).
Small-Cap Stock	A small-cap stock is issued by a small company. It is often considered speculative (high-risk).
Penny Stock	A penny stock usually sells for less than $1 a share. This stock is issued by new companies or highly risky companies. You can make big money if the company does well. However, the stock will be worthless if the company fails.

Directions: Before buying a stock, investors must select an investing strategy. For example, they may decide to buy medium-risk growth stocks and hold them for several years. They might decide to buy income stocks that pay high dividends. Investors' choices will reflect their needs and what they think about the economy and the prospects for certain companies. They will also reflect the risks investors are willing to take. Read about each of the investors below. Using the stock descriptions on the previous page, make recommendations about an investing strategy for each investor.

1. Miguel is making his first stock purchase. He has some other investments, mostly safe and liquid ones. Which type of stock do you think Miguel should buy? Why do you recommend this choice?

2. Hanae is seeking more risk and larger returns for 20 years from now. Which type of stock do you think she should buy? Why do you recommend this choice?

3. Larry is retired. Which type of stock do you think he should buy? Why do you recommend this choice?

4. Linda has inherited a large amount of money. She wants to invest it and is willing to take moderate risk. Which type of stock do you think she should buy? Why do you recommend this choice?